WHAT PEOPLE ARE SAYING ABOUT START PLANTING!

"As I read *Start Planting!* it became clear to me that Mr. Thomas is doing anointed work. This book transforms our everyday Christian understanding of what it means to create wealth and why wealth creation is intertwined with being a child of God. Using insights that will empower readers, the book skillfully shows that applying the principles of investing and creating wealth is something we are all able to do."

—Damon J. Phillips, Ph.D., Associate Professor,
The University of Chicago Graduate School of Business

"The role of money in the Christian lifestyle can be a confusing subject, with people offering opinions that range from limited to self-serving. In *Stop Digging!* and *Start Planting!*, Ministers Thomas and Goins get it right. They provide for us a model for personal financial success through the application of impeccable educational and professional credentials, real world financial sector experience and perspectives that can only be described as anointed. They give readers a roadmap to personal wealth that is in lockstep with the Christian walk by keeping money in its proper place. They definitely show that we don't have to be 'of the world' in order to find fulfillment and success 'in the world'. I recommend this series of guides to everyone."

—Darrell Williams, Chief Investment Officer,
Telecommunications Development Fund

"I don't know about others, but as a Christian, I have personally struggled with the issue of accumulating money and other assets. *Start Planting!* is a tremendous resource in understanding why it's 'ok' to use your God-given mind and talents to succeed in investing and capitalizing on business opportunities. This book will help many to understand that when you have the proper relationship with God any and all things are possible. *Start Planting!* is a cadre of sunshine, water, and nutrients destined to help many individuals grow their financial gardens."

—Mattie D. Blair, MBA, President and CEO,
BSG Training & Consulting, Inc.

D1279875

"Despite my years of investing experience, Shundrawn's novel approach helped me discover new ways of looking at investing. It's not easy to teach an experienced investor new tricks... but I guess that gives you an idea of just how insightful this book is."
—*Eric T. McKissack, CFA, former Vice Chairman and Portfolio Manager, Ariel Capital Management, Inc.*

"What an inspiration! I have rarely experienced a book that couples two of the subjects that I feel most passionate about: Investing and Christ. This goes at the top of the lists of 'Life's Lessons'. Thank you, Shundrawn!"
—*Nicole Pullen Ross, Vice President, Investment Management Group at a Global Investment Bank*

"The financial services industry has taken great efforts to confuse the public. The confusion is now so great that people have been driven to indecision. It is refreshing to see a new common sense approach to thinking about finance. Kudos to the authors of *Stop Digging!* and *Start Planting!*"
—*Lyle Logan, Senior Vice President, The Northern Trust Company*

"*Start Planting!* is not only financially sound but more importantly is Biblically sound. Practical advice on managing your finances and creating wealth in a manner that honors Christ. This book will bless you both financially and spiritually.
—*Jonathan Mueller, CFA, CPA, Equity Analyst, AIM Investments*

"*Start Planting!* in very simple terms, clarifies to all investors that you don't need a lot of money to become wealthy."
—*Van Hutcherson, Managing Director, Equities Division at a Global Investment Bank*

ADELPHOS

START
PLANTING!

To Dr. & Mrs. Dollar,

May God continue to use you mightily to empower and enlighten His people. As a carpenter, Made in the image and likeness of the great carpenter, I know that you will continue to teach others how to lead a truly abundant life. Carsor Thomas Abraham A. Thomas 6/10/03

$\mathcal{S}$TART
PLANTING!

A Spiritual Guide to Wealth
Creation and Successful Investing

SHUNDRAWN A. THOMAS

Unless otherwise noted, all Scripture taken from the King James Version.

This publication contains the opinions and ideas of its author and is designed to provide useful information in regard to the subject matter covered. It is sold with the understanding that the publisher is not engaged in rendering legal, financial, tax preparation, or other professional services. Laws vary from state to state, and if the reader requires expert assistance or legal advice, a competent professional should be consulted. Readers should not rely on this (or any other) publication for financial guidance, but should do their own homework and make their own decisions. The author and publisher specifically disclaim any responsibility for any liability, loss, or risk, personal or otherwise, which is incurred as a consequence, directly or indirectly, of the use and application of any of the contents of this book.

Cover illustration by Emily Costa.
Cover and interior design by Pneuma Books, LLC.
For more information, visit www.pneumabooks.com

Distributed by Bookworld Companies
1941 Whitfield Park Loop, Sarasota, FL 34243
www.bookworld.com

Publisher's Cataloging-in-Publication
(Provided by Quality Books, Inc.)

Thomas, Shundrawn A.
   Start Planting : a spiritual guide to wealth creation
and successful investing / Shundrawn A. Thomas. -- 1st ed.
   p. cm. -- (Adelphos Publishing's economic empowerment
series ; 2)
   LCCN 2002096932
   ISBN 0-9727418-1-x

   1. Investments--Religious aspects--Chrisitanity.
   2. Finance, Personal--Religious aspects--Christianity.
   3. Christians--Finance, Personal.   I. Title II. Title:
Start planting

HG4521.T467 2003   332.6
                 QBI03-200046

      10 09 08 07 06 05 04 03   6 5 4 3 2 1

Start (verb) — to begin activity or operation; to begin work (especially suddenly); to bring into being.

Planting (verb tense) — the act of sowing seeds or setting in the ground for growth; the act of establishing.

DEDICATION

*This book is dedicated to Adam and Eve,
the couple that managed their resources so poorly
that they literally lost the entire world.*

*This book is dedicated to God Almighty, who loved
Adam and Eve so much that He gave His Word
to restore all that they lost.*

*And, this book is dedicated to you, the reader.
May God's promise of restoration to Adam and Eve
be fulfilled through you.*

ACKNOWLEDGMENTS

First, giving praise to my Lord and Savior, Jesus Christ, for the gift of abundant life. In this endeavor and in all endeavors I acknowledge Him because He directs my path.

To my soul mate, Latania, and our beautiful son, Javon. I thank you both for your perfect love and your unfaltering support. Latania, time and words would fail if I tried to express the love I have for you. Javon and I are truly blessed.

To my soul brother, Cliff, and your beautiful wife, Janelle. I thank you both for your words of wisdom, gestures of encouragement, and acts of love. Cliff, God has called us for such a time as this. Continue to stir up the gifts that are in you.

To my pastors and parents, Gary and Audrey Thomas. Everyone needs a God that they can see. Thank you for allowing me to see God through you. I love you both dearly.

To my darling sister, Saeyonniea. I have watched you mature into a truly virtuous woman. You will always be our baby girl. I love you little lady.

To my brothers, Michael and Jarreon. There is no relation closer than brothers. I'm privileged to have two mighty men of God like you to share that relationship with. I love you both.

To my network-The Thomas family; The Austin and Brandon families; my in-laws, Carlos, Verbue, Nicco, and Vashti; the fellas, Gregory, Cecyl, Richard, Theadius, Michael, Cedric, Stacy, Dale, Tirrell, and Trevoir; the Beta Nu brothers of Alpha Phi Alpha; the FAMU Rattler Family; Sue Toigo and the entire Toigo Family; my professional mentors, Jim Reynolds, Lyle Logan, Eric McKissack, and Keith Cooper; Pneuma Books; and Liquid Soul Media. Thank you for believing in me.

To the Look Up & Live family as well as my extended family and friends. Thank you for your prayers and support.

Start Planting!

To the men and women of God who have sown the seeds of righteousness into my life — Pastor George Liggins, Maimie Till Mobley, Pearl Brandon (Grandma), Pastors Carlton and Paul Arthurs, Pastor Derrick Jackson, Dr. Myles Munroe, Pastor John Cherry, Pastors Randy and Paula White, Pastor Scott Thomas, Dr. James Dobson, Jim and Elizabeth George, Stormie Omaritan, Minister Mark Holiday and Minister Brian Marshall. God bless you and keep you.

To everyone that purchases this book, thank you for supporting the vision.

Contents

Part III   Types of Investments

Part IV   Appendices

∽

FOREWORD

Who Am I?

I am just a regular Joe. I happen to like the subject of investments. I feel like I should have much more wealth right now than I do. (Who doesn't?) I believe God created the concept of investing, so He should have some suggestions about what I should do with my resources. Right? I am seeking to find what the Bible says about investing. In addition to reading the Bible itself, I like to read what God's children have to say about investing. I also like to read what investment professionals have to say about investing. It is particularly helpful when I can learn from an investment professional who is God's child. Then I can get a two-fer! I firmly trust that God has put every foundational idea I need to effectively create wealth and successfully invest resources in His Word. Furthermore, I know that He has given apostles, evangelists, prophets, pastors, and teachers as gifts in the body of Christ that I may become mature in my financial life through His Word.

Who Are You?

You are probably just like me. You picked up this book because you want to learn something that will assist you in becoming wealthy. You picked up this book because you are interested in God's perspective on investing. You picked up this book because your pastor, your friend, or a family member recommended it. You picked up this book because God destined you to read it and ordained it to forever transform your life. Unfortunately, you are probably still stuck with the 95 percent of people that only control 5 percent of the wealth in the world. You are trying to remedy that situation. You keep reading and hearing all this great stuff about God and how His people should be prosperous, but you have yet to master the fine points of making that happen. You might not even recognize that you have to be taught how to live a prosperous life, because prosperous thinking does not come automatically for most people. Prosperity begins with achieving financial freedom and embracing sound stewardship. It continues by building your knowledge of the difference between producing assets and generating liabilities. Prosperity blossoms when you learn how to create wealth and invest successfully.

Who Is Shundrawn A. Thomas?

Shundrawn is a regular Joe just like us. And Shundrawn is a gifted teacher. He is a son of God, a father, a husband, a brother, a friend, an investment professional, a minister, an author, an entrepreneur, and a motivational speaker. He is an up and coming real estate mogul. He is a vessel meet for the Master's use. *Start Planting!* is literally his launching pad into an even greater ministry directed and funded by the Holy Spirit. He is destined to preach and teach all over the world breaking the Truth of God down into practical, bite-sized pieces. He is anything but traditional; he's a revolutionary, if you will. God has given him an awesome word concerning the link between God's financial philosophy and the concept of investing. The foundational overview in this book will prepare you to have good success in the areas of wealth creation and successful investing. *Start Planting!* is a seed of increase ready to explode in your life. This book will teach you God's outlook on investing, principles of investing, and the different types of investments. May you be even more enlightened and changed than I was as you digest part two of *Adelphos Publishing's Economic Empowerment Series, Start Planting!*

Faithfully Yours,
Cliff "Tony" Goins IV, CPA
Author, *Stop Digging! A Spiritual Guide to Financial Freedom and Sound Stewardship*

PREFACE

Phil. 3:13-14 "Brethren, I count not myself to have apprehended: but this one thing I do, forgetting those things that are behind and reaching forth unto those things which are before, I press toward the mark for the prize of the high calling of God in Christ Jesus."

The Apostle Paul is arguably the greatest evangelist and one of the greatest teachers the world has ever known. The books that Paul penned make up the majority of the New Testament and serve as the foundation of most Christian doctrine. In this brief excerpt from Paul's letter to the church at Philippi, Paul shares some intimate thoughts with his brothers and sisters in Christ. It is believed that Paul penned this letter while imprisoned in Rome around 60-62 A.D. Paul suggested that he had not accomplished everything God had called him to do or become everything God had called him to be. This is a peculiar statement coming from this great man of

God. After all, this statement was made after his three missionary journeys, approximately 15 years into his ministry.

In spite of all Paul had accomplished, he was motivated to move on to new challenges. Paul did not dwell on his shortcomings, instead he constantly worked on building his character. Above all, there was one thing he was intensely focused on. His ultimate goal was to fulfill the purpose that God planned for his life and to fully employ his gifts, talents, and abilities. He was so focused on achieving this goal that he wrote this letter of encouragement while he himself was imprisoned. Paul understood that as long as he was in the will of God, nothing could stop God's plan for his life.

By this time you are probably wondering how this passage of scripture relates to creating wealth. I will save you the trouble of wondering. It doesn't! Although it doesn't directly pertain to wealth or financial independence, it is pertinent. This scripture is meant to tell you a little bit about me and hopefully a little bit about yourself. Since we will be spending a bit of time together (nine chapters to be exact), I thought I'd introduce myself. I want to start by stating that I am a born-again believer. I believe that God's Word was made flesh and came into this world as the Son of Man. I believe that Jesus was born of a virgin and lived without sin. I believe He was crucified for the sins of the world and was resurrected from the grave with all power and authority. I have accepted Jesus as my Lord and personal Savior and the life that I now live belongs to Him. Now there are many other things that I could tell you about myself, but professing to be a born again believer is the most revealing. And since you probably didn't pick up this text to read my autobiography, I want to focus on what is important and essential.

Like Paul, I am intensely focused on achieving the purpose God has for my life. I believe that if you are reading this text you have the same desire. That is why we are meeting here — between the covers of this book. I believe that no meeting is by chance. So whether you purchased this book, received it as a gift, or borrowed a copy from a friend, you are meant to read this book. Creating wealth is largely dependent on your ability to fully employ the gifts, talents, and abilities that God has sown into you. Creating wealth is also dependent on your willingness to sow the seeds of knowledge found in the Word of God into your everyday life. This book illuminates one of the most elementary principles found in the Bible — the principle of sowing and reaping. Just as I hope to sow into your life by sharing what God has revealed to me through His Word, you are sowing into my life by taking the time to read this book. I thank you from the bottom of my heart for supporting the vision that God has given me. And I pray that God will fulfill the desires of your heart and reveal to you those things that you were in search of when you picked up this book.

INTRODUCTION

THERE IS MORE TO LIFE THAN MONEY!

We often take the power of God's Word for granted. But if you think of the Bible as God's thoughts revealed, you will not do so. I have learned over time that the Bible is so profound that the revelations contained within its covers are endless. When Jesus talked about whom man would serve, He only mentioned two entities: God and mammon, which is money. My father, who is a pastor, always notes that God specifically left out the devil, which suggests that our greatest challenge is dealing with money. Even more disconcerting, it suggests that individuals can go as far as to allow money to become their god.

If the true living God is your God, you will still have a relationship with mammon. The question is what that relationship will be. God gave man (mankind) authority in the earth, which means we are called to dominate. Every resource in the earth is at man's disposal (that's you!), and was provided for the express purpose of accomplishing God's vision in the earth. Now stay with me because this is deep. Money is merely a medium of exchange. It allows for the transfer of goods. In other words, it is just a claim on some stuff. The money in your wallet, in your bank account, or under your mattress, merely represents your claim on some of the resources that God gave to man. Now here is the kicker! When Jesus talks about mammon being man's god (Matt. 6:24), He is essentially saying that many of us have gotten so far out of position that the things we were given to have dominion over are now controlling us. I don't know what you think, but that's pretty deep to me.

Now that we have gotten that money thing out of the way, we can really talk. What I want to convey through this book is so much bigger than money. This book is about resources. Now if you read it carefully, you realized that *Stop Digging!* was about resources. More specifically, it addressed how to be a good steward over your God-given resources. Assuming you have an understanding of how to live debt free and how to be a good steward over your resources, it is time to address what God's intention was when He gave man all these wonderful resources.

Why did God create man? What is man's purpose here on earth? I believe the answers to these essential questions are revealed in the first two chapters of Genesis. As a matter of fact, I would even recommend pausing here to review Genesis 1 and 2 if you haven't read them lately. These chapters are vital because they talk about man before the fall. They reveal what God created us to be and not what we became — but that's another book.

> *Gen. 2:8* "And the Lord God planted a garden eastward in Eden; and there He put (think *planted*) the man He had formed."

This scripture is profound. It tells us that man is God's seed, which He planted in the Garden of Eden. You will find several definitions for the word *Eden*. Roughly translated, it means point or place. In our modern dictionaries we see the word associated with or defined as paradise. I think there is some utility in both of these definitions. God planted man in the earth as a seed, which God fully expects to reproduce and bring forth fruit. God planted man in the fertile soil of Eden. Now the reason Eden is accurately defined as a point or place is because God's intention was for man to replenish the earth, or, in other words, make the whole world just like Eden. Man was God's greatest creation and man was also the choicest seed God planted in the earth. So, among other things, God is a great gardener. We know that we are made in God's image and likeness, which means that God expects us to be great gardeners as well. God expects us to plant the resources that He has given us in fertile ground so that they will bring forth an abundant harvest.

God not only expects us to be good stewards, but He commanded us to multiply our resources and recreate His vision for the earth. My objective, through the direction of the Holy Spirit, is to build a foundation of sound spiritual principles. These principles, if applied faithfully, will allow the believer to multiply his or her resources, as well as produce good natural and spiritual fruit. In short, I want to change your way of thinking to what we at Adelphos refer to as the planter mentality. So now that you have put an end to digging, allow God to work through you and start planting. May God bless the harvest.

PART I

WHAT GOD WANTS YOU TO KNOW ABOUT INVESTING

CHAPTER 1

CREATING WEALTH

A Lesson from a Father to a Son

Whether You Admit It or Not, Money Matters...

Why do so many of us falter when it comes to achieving financial goals and creating wealth? While I'm sure there are individuals who have no desire to be wealthy, I haven't met many of them. Most people I meet, given the choice, would just as soon have wealth than not. There's certainly no shortage of advice on how to achieve financial independence. You've seen all the books. There's *Think and Grow Rich*, *Rich Dad, Poor Dad*, and *The Craft of Investing*. For what it's worth, I think these are all good reads. Given the sheer volume written on the subject matter, you'd figure we would all be rich, or at least two to three chapters from getting there. Alas, creating wealth seems to elude most of us, or about 95 percent of the world's population. But who's counting!

Have You Lost Your Mind Yet?

The Holy Spirit revealed something to me that is strikingly simple yet strikingly true. The vast majority of people lack the ability to create wealth because, quite frankly, they lack creativity. That is exactly why you can't create wealth by just reading a book. Reading gives you access to knowledge. However, knowledge is useless without a proper vision. Your vision allows you to take something known - knowledge — and change it into something unknown — a new creation. If you want a bona fide breakthrough in this area, I recommend you pick up a copy of Dr. Myles Munroe's book *Releasing Your Potential*, but enough with my commercials.

Prov. 29:18 "Where there is no vision, the people perish."

If you really want to get anywhere in this world, you can't trust your mind. In fact, I am going to ask you to lose your mind right now. Isn't that what the Bible asks?

Phil. 2:5 "Let this mind be in you, that was also in Christ Jesus."

Those who are born again should appreciate the potential of a renewed mind. Your mind is like a computer. It merely processes things, both good and bad. Creativity comes not from your mind but from your spirit. Full utilization of your creativity requires the right relationship with God, your Creator. Since God created you, He knows all your creative abilities. After all, He gave them to you. If you are born again, your spirit is alive and your spirit is what connects you to God your Creator. A born again spirit can utilize a renewed mind to process the wonderful visions we receive from God. And this, my brothers and sisters, is the first lesson of many regarding the creation of wealth.

Father Knows Best

I want to get the ball rolling with a bold statement. Creation is not just about God and man. Creation is also about God and His Son. My father/pastor told me something years ago that only fully resonates now. The first thing that God begot or gave birth to was His Word (Son). Why is this important? Because with this thought in mind, I would like to suggest that Creation can be viewed as a lesson from a father to a son. This critical teaching is the lesson of creating wealth and investing. If we can truly see the lesson that the Word teaches us through the account of Creation, we can better understand what God expects of us. Furthermore, I believe in my heart that we must teach this lesson to our children. By children I mean to our natural children as well as those whom we have led to Christ and fellow believers in our circle of influence.

What is this lesson I keep alluding to? We have to begin with scripture, so you may want to grab your Bibles and turn to John 1. I am going to reference this chapter as well as interject some thoughts for emphasis. The most important thing to bear in mind is that whenever you see a reference to *the Word*; it is referring to Jesus Christ, the Son of God.

> *John 1:1-3* "In the beginning was the Word (the Son), and the Word (the Son) was with God (the Father). The same (the Son) was in the beginning with God (the Father). All things were made by Him (the Son); and without Him (the Son) was not anything made that was made."

This passage provides several key revelations. It tells us plainly that God's Word, His Son, was with Him from the very beginning. We find that not only was the Son present during creation, but that everything was actually made by the Son. The operative word here is *made*. When I read Genesis, I picture God with a vision or a blueprint of heaven and earth. He imparts this vision to His Son who

3

then goes out and makes all the things that the Father created or de-signed. God (the Father) did not allow anything to be made with-out the Word (His Son).

If Genesis states that God created heaven and earth, then how did His Son make everything? I am going to explain it two ways. First, you can't separate God from His Word. That is why Jesus told Phillip if you have seen me you have seen the Father (John 14:9). You could look at it as if they made everything together. But let's take it a step further. The Bible uses very specific words. It states that God *creat-ed* heaven and earth. How many people know that the creator of something isn't necessarily the individual who makes it? Architects create buildings but never lay one brick. Engineers design cars but usually don't build them. Thus the Son, like a faithful child, learned from His Father, the Creator. We will observe in a later chapter what a good study the Son is.

The First Lesson

The first lesson that God taught His Son was how to create wealth. After all, what is wealth? The dictionary defines *wealth* as an abun-dance of riches, resources, or valuable possessions. Two scriptures help make this point clear: Gen. 1:1, "In the beginning God created the heaven and the earth"; and John 1:1, "In the beginning was the Word and the Word was with God." With God's vision and guidance, His Word went out and made the heavens and the earth. He set in place the magnificent sun that lights the sky by day and the luminous moon and stars that light the sky by night. He provided an abundance of water sufficient for every living thing and a complex ecosystem whereby all organisms work together to sustain one another. He made lush vegetation, some of which is good for food and other types that help produce life-giving oxygen. He made the beautiful birds that soar through the air. He made the intriguing fish of the sea. And He made the many wondrous creatures that creep about the earth.

My guess is that some of you may be struggling with my reference to "the Creation" as the generation of wealth. Let's take a closer look at wealth.

Wealth and Money Are Not the Same!

Wealthy people understand that wealth and money are different. Wealthy people generally have a lot of money, but they understand that money alone does not make them wealthy. In fact, you can still qualify as a wealthy individual without any money in your pocket or in your bank account. See, there is this little term called inflation. In basic terms, inflation means that money is worth a little bit less every day. Because of inflation, money doesn't retain value very well. People who walk around with lots of money in their pocket aren't necessarily wealthy. They are generally ill informed or even foolish. A fact little known among the have-nots is that the world's wealthiest people derive much of their wealth from owning real estate. They merely laid claim on a piece of God's green earth, which He gave man dominion over.

Individuals who are truly wealthy are also careful to store wealth in assets other than real estate. Stocks and bonds, rare artwork (which is merely another person's creation), and jewelry are commonly used to store wealth. Recall that John 1:3 states that "all things" were made by the Son. "All things" refers to the heaven and earth that God created in Genesis. If the heavens and earth as well as everything that lies within them do not qualify as wealth, then I don't know what does.

Your True Inheritance

For all those who can't accept that God wants believers to generate wealth, again I enter the book of Genesis into the court record. God started by creating... well... everything. His Word grabbed a hold of the vision and made not just a whole lot of things — He made *everything*. Now along comes man who is made in the image and likeness of God. Why would God expect us to do anything less than generate wealth? God wants us to acquire wealth. He made everything for us. Please read your Bibles closely! The scripture states that *the love of money* is the root of all evil (1 Tim. 6:10). This scripture pertains to having the proper relationship with money. Problems arise when we let wealth or things get in the way of our relationship with God.

Consider this: Gen 1:26 states that God gave man dominion over all the earth. In other words, man inherited a lot of stuff. If you have time, go outside or go to a window and look around. Everything as far as your eyes can see — and much more — are part of your inheritance. It's that simple. But the first rule to laying claim to your inheritance is that you must be part of the family. The second rule is that you must be in right standing with the benefactor. When you have the right relationship with God, you have an abundant claim on the things of this world and the world to come. Some of us don't take the Bible seriously when it says we are joint heirs with Christ. Most of the world's wealth is inherited rather than generated. This is why wealthy individuals focus much of their financial planning around preserving wealth and not generating it, because generating wealth requires taking risks.

God's Property

To develop a proper attitude toward wealth, we must understand certain spiritual principles. Many wealthy people are spiritually bankrupt. While they may have a lot of the nice things we associate with happiness, they often feel empty inside. The objective of this book is for you to acquire the right things both inside and out. If you have all the riches in the world but don't have a relationship with God, you can't experience the joy of His love. Without a relationship with God the Creator, it is also impossible to achieve true success because success is achieved by doing what you were created to do. While God loves all of mankind, God is holy. As such, God cannot associate Himself with sin. We sin when we make choices outside the will of God. When you are out of the will of God, you are in effect choosing not to have a relationship with the Father. How does this apply to acquiring wealth?

> *Deut. 8:18* "Thou shalt remember the Lord thy God: for it is He that giveth thee power to get wealth, that He might establish His covenant, which He sware unto thy fathers"

Some of you may be wondering why sinners seem to acquire lots of wealth. Or you may believe that everything you own, you acquired yourself. Both of these ideas suggest that God has nothing to do with the acquisition of wealth. Let's see what the Word has to say about these views.

In 1 Cor. 10:26, we learn that the earth is the Lord's and the fullness thereof. That means no one can acquire anything in the earth unless God permits it. The things of God, which are eternal, cannot be acquired unless we have the right relationship with God. However, the things of this world, which are temporal, are accessible to saved and sinner alike. If an individual works for these things, he or she can acquire them. The operative word here is *work*. You can't just wish for them, and for all you holy rollers, you can't just pray for them either. Faith without works is dead (James 2:20).

The Bible also tells us that the gifts and calling of God are without repentance (Rom. 11:29). That means God won't take them back. God has given gifts to all mankind for both natural and spiritual gain. Whether we use our gifts to the glory of God or not, they will produce when called upon. This is why people who have gifts such as writing, singing, speaking, or painting are able to use these for

7

their gain. So our primary means of acquiring things in the earth is good old-fashioned hard work. If we want to produce anything, we must be willing to work. With respect to sinners acquiring wealth, the Bible is clear on this issue.

> *Prov. 13: 21-22* "Evil pursueth sinners: but to the righteous good shall be repayed. A good man leaveth an inheritance for his children's children and the wealth of the sinner is laid up for the just."

While it may seem that those who are outside of the will of God continue to prosper, it is only for a season. Their wealth is merely being stored up for the believer. If you trust God enough to allow Him to lead you, you can go out and claim your inheritance.

The True Definition of Wealth

We already know how the dictionary defines wealth. How should believers define it? Mal. 3:10 tells us that if we are faithful and render to God what is His, then He will open up the windows of heaven, and pour out a blessing that we don't have room enough to receive. This manifold blessing that the Bible is referring to isn't money, rather it is the abundance of spiritual resources we have access to as born again believers. (I have Pastor John Cherry to thank for this revelation.) Our greatest wealth comes not from the material things God allows us to acquire, but the spiritual resources we have access to when we have God's Spirit living on the inside.

> *Eph. 2: 4-7* "But God, who is rich in mercy, for His great love wherewith He loved us, even when we were dead in sins, hath quickened us together, and made us sit together in heavenly places in Christ Jesus: That in the ages to come He might show us the exceeding

riches of His grace in His kindness toward us through
Christ Jesus."

This scripture reveals the true origin of our wealth as believers. God
not only has mercy on us and invites us into His royal family, but He
allows His grace to operate in our lives. My father/pastor provided
me with a great definition for grace. He told me that grace is all of
God's power and attributes working on our behalf. This grace ensures that we become all that God has called us to be. It dawned on
me that this is the reason the scripture uses the term exceeding riches of His grace. Now that's powerful.

In addition to God's grace operating in our lives, we enjoy other
types of spiritual wealth. When we allow God to lead us, we take on
His character and the fruits of the Spirit are produced in our lives.
These are love, joy, peace, longsuffering, gentleness, goodness, faith,
meekness, and temperance (Gal. 5:22). These characteristics are evidence that the Holy Spirit lives in us. The blessings that flow from
this spiritual fruit represent the true wealth we acquire when we live
according to the Word of God. Bottom line, believers should teach
their children that God is the source of all wealth. If we truly seek
His will for our lives and tap into the Creator's creativity, we can expect to grow wealthy both naturally and spiritually.

Start Planting!

SEEDS FOR YOUR SOIL

The Mind of Christ : Phil. 2:1-8

1. How should we treat other believers?

2. What does it mean to have the mind of Christ?

3. What character traits does the mind of Christ produce?

The Word of God : John 1:1-5

1. Who is the Word of God?

2. What did the Word of God make?

3. What does the Word of God give us?

A Father's Instruction: Proverbs 13

1. What distinguishes a wise individual?

2. What can diligent individuals look forward to?

3. What should we expect when we refuse godly instruction?

4. What distinguishes a good financial steward?

5. What happens to the wealth of sinners?

CHAPTER 2

EMPOWERED NOT EMPLOYED

Why Your True Calling Is to Be an Investor and Not an Employee

It Was a Dirty Job and God Loved Us Enough to Do It!

As I read Genesis and countless scriptures in the Bible, the revelation that the Holy Spirit gave me is that God is an investor. The term *invest* carries several definitions. It means to furnish with authority and power. It also means to supply someone or something with resources in expectation of reaping a return.

> *Gen. 1:26-28* "And God said, Let us make man in our image, after our likeness: and let them have dominion over the fish of the sea, and over the fowl of the air, and over the cattle, and over all the earth, and over every creeping thing that creepeth upon the earth. So God created man in His image, in the image of God created He him; male and female created He them. And God blessed them, and said unto them, Be fruitful and multiply, and replenish the earth, and subdue it:"

When you read Genesis both of these definitions come into play. In Gen. 1:26 God furnishes man with power ("let us make man in our image") and authority ("and let them have dominion"... over all the earth). We also see that God expects a return on His invested resources when He instructs man in Gen. 1:28 to "be fruitful, multiply and replenish the earth." Remember, when God refers to man, you should read it as mankind (male and female). This is why Gen. 1:26 reads, "let them have dominion"; and Gen. 1:28 reads, "and God blessed them." Bottom line: this teaching applies to men and women alike.

Look how important man is to God. For every creation, except man, God spoke and the Word brought it into being. When it came down to man, the Father decided to personally get involved. The Father spoke to His Word and His Spirit and said that together they would make man in their image. In Gen. 1:27 the Trinity went to the drawing board and created both male and female in their image. It doesn't stop there. Fast forward to Gen. 2:7 and it says that the Father Himself formed man from the dust of the ground. You could figuratively say that He rolled up His sleeves and got His hands dirty. So to stick with our analogy, here we have the Father with His Son at His side fashioning the man He created. Notice that man was formed from the dust of the earth, representing the symbiotic relationship that man has with everything in the earth.

Who's the Boss?

When we speak of the relationship that man has with everything in the earth we can sum it up in one word: dominion. God gave man authority in the earth. God respects His decision so much that He doesn't do anything in the earth without the permission of a man. Any spirit, even an evil spirit, has to work through people to accomplish anything in the earth. That is why we must be born again. Only through spiritual rebirth can the Holy Spirit lead us. God has given us the freedom of choice, but He fully expects us to choose to do His will. How does that apply here? It's quite simple. God never intended for you to work for anyone but Him. I am going to repeat that. God never intended for you to work for anyone but Him! Now my guess is that many of you spend the majority of your time working for someone who does not wear the title Lord of Lords and King of Kings. Even as I write this book I work twelve-hour days on what I like to refer to as my part-time job.

I know what you're thinking. How can you afford to quit your job and go to work for God? After all, there are bills to pay. Should we all become entrepreneurs? Don't all entrepreneurs need employees? The answer is more straightforward than you might think. I am not suggesting that you will never be employed. In fact, it is likely that many of us will labor on a job. We should not despise this time, but instead work diligently, serving others. What we refer to as work is generally not our life's work. If we are born again, we have been bought with a price (1 Cor. 7:23). Paul understood this and this is why Paul referred to himself as a bondservant. Our life's work is to serve God and fulfill the calling that God has on our lives.

Our jobs provide a means of sustaining our families and ourselves and afford us resources that enable us to work for God. I went to my job for approximately twelve hours today so that I could come home and work on this book, which is part of my life's work. If we allow the Spirit to lead us, we often find occupations that are fulfilling because they tie into the plan that God has for our lives. I work in financial services. My career choice has armed me with many experiences that are helpful in writing this book. If we are obedient to the Word, God can use our job experiences to both educate and develop us. It is through work that we discover our gifts, talents, and abilities. So we should always give our best. The key is to understand that while an individual may employ you, you ultimately work for and answer to God.

You've Got to Plant Your Own Garden

Now that I have given you the speech about being a great employee, I am going to help you see that your true calling is not to remain an employee. I know... I've pulled the rug right out from under you. Let's start with a cold hard fact. People don't employ others to make those individuals wealthy. Entrepreneurs are impregnated with a seed that they want to turn into a harvest for themselves. They employ other individuals because they have a vision. So they rent the talents of their employees and have those employees contribute to that vision. The visionary or the creator is the chief beneficiary and reaps the profits from the vision. This is why entrepreneurs become rich and their employees earn wages. Now this may seem insensitive, but it is both sensible and scriptural.

> *Isa. 55:10* "For the rain cometh down, and the snow
> from heaven, and returneth not thither, but watereth
> the earth, and maketh it bring forth bud, that it may
> give seed to the sower, and bread to the eater."

The increase of seeds goes to the sower. When you see the word *sower*, you should think visionary or entrepreneur. Notice that it doesn't say that the increase goes to the reaper, which would be the employee. We all come here full of seeds, but we must seek God for the vision He has for our lives. To really make sense out of all of this, I want to take you back to the book of Genesis to examine how God establishes order.

> *Gen. 2:15* "And the Lord God took the man, and put
> him into the Garden of Eden to dress it and keep it."

After He made man, God gave him a job to do. (This was before the woman was formed and before the fall.) So make no bones about it:

God always intended for man to work. But here comes the good part — the job was not man's calling. Mankind received their calling in the *first* chapter of Genesis: Be fruitful, multiply, and replenish the earth. In other words, the job that the man received in Gen. 2:15 was merely an assignment. (Women, if your man is not employed you have every right to tell him to go out and get a job!)

Responsibility Will Make a Man (or Woman) Out of You!

God needed to give man some responsibility before He gave him a family and before man moved on to his true destiny or calling. The same thing happens on your job. You are generally given a series of assignments with increasing responsibility. It is only after gaining the necessary experience that you move on to management. So while you may be hired on the management tract, you begin with an assignment. See, God looks at our end and then starts us at the beginning. God called Adam to be an investor. Man's charge was to replenish the earth — in other words, make the whole earth like paradise. The upkeep of Eden was just an assignment on the way to his true calling. Slight problem! Adam failed his first assignment. So we've had a six-thousand-year diversion, but who's counting.

The Bible provides numerous examples of the relationship between work and calling. When Moses fled from Egypt, Jethro, a Midianite shepherd-priest, took him in (Exod. 2:21). Moses married Jethro's daughter and subsequently worked tending Jethro's flock. Although Moses was called to be a deliverer, Jethro was his employer for forty years (Exod. 3:1). I believe that during this time God was preparing Moses and sowing into him the things that he would need to fulfill his calling. If you examine Moses' relationship with Jethro, you will find that he had tremendous respect for his father-in-law and served him faithfully. Because of his faithful service, God mightily used him. The take-away is simple: your calling is far greater than your assignment. We must allow God to develop us through our work and seek Him for the purpose He has for our lives. Think about how different the world would be if we applied these simple principles. Imagine if we had men who worked and established a home before getting married; or men who learned to deal with responsibility before starting a family. Imagine if we could just learn to be obedient and truly submissive to God as opposed to faltering at simple assignments. Sounds like a dream? Actually it's God's vision for man.

God's Attitude toward Investing

> *Eph. 3:20-21* "Now unto Him (God) that is able to do exceedingly, abundantly above all we ask or think, according to the power that worketh in us, unto Him be glory in the church by Christ Jesus throughout all ages"

Remember, man is God's choicest seed. God planted one man in the earth and today the earth is inhabited by more than six billion people inhabiting the earth. Talk about being fruitful and multiplying! This is not to mention the animal populations, vegetation, and countless other investments that God has caused to produce abundant returns. That is why Eph. 3:20 states that God is able to do "exceeding abundantly above all we ask or think." So I think the record proves that God is the greatest investor. Stating that God is the greatest anything is hardly controversial. However, it is only through careful study that we realize what a truly wonderful investor God is.

When God blew into the man He had formed, He gave the body life by injecting His Spirit. With God's Spirit on the inside, the man was impregnated with God's vision for the earth. This was prior to the introduction of sin, so man's spirit was fully functional and in constant contact with the Father. When God planted the man in the Garden (Gen. 2:8), He made an investment in the earth — an investment that God fully expects to reap a return on! Everything that

God wanted out of the world was in that one seed, man. As with all seed's, God created man to give Him an exponential return.

What God Taught Mankind about Investing

Expecting a return is obviously not what makes God an investor. Plenty of individuals expect a return - but often they want something for nothing. They may not express that verbally, but they express it through their actions. Many people show up to church every week and act as spectators. They never sow into the ministry or contribute their talents and abilities. God doesn't operate that way - and neither should you. When God wants an abundant return He begins by making an investment. That's what He did when He created man. Many people read the book of Genesis and envision God taking man from the earth, when in reality He planted man in the earth. The only way that the earth can truly give God the abundant return that it was meant to yield is through man. Man is a necessary investment charged with bringing forth God's vision.

> *Gen. 2:2* "And on the seventh day God ended His work which He had made; and He rested on the seventh day from all His work which He had made."

Isn't that awesome? God established the principles of investing in the very beginning. God's investment was so incredible that He only had to make one deposit. Everything He desired was inside the man that He planted in the Garden. Why do you think God rested on the seventh day? Once God's vision was sown into the earth, all God had to do was sit back and let man carry out His plan. If we look at it another way, there was nothing in the earth with God's vision prior to man. So the earth was full of potential, but only man could bring it forth. That is why God gave man dominion. That is also why "Creation" ended with man.

Getting Your Resources to Work for You

Gen. 2:3 "And God blessed the seventh day and sanctified it; because that in it He had rested from all His work which God created and made."

I believe the seventh day was blessed because God could now begin to reap returns from His investment. During the first six days of creation, God was hard at work creating resources and preparing a place for man. Notice that God did not make the whole world a paradise, only Eden. He didn't fill the earth with living things, but put seeds in all He created so they could reproduce after themselves. It's as if God spent six days working and saving up. God was showing us how to get our resources to work for us. Once He was satisfied that the necessary investment had been made, He went from a state of work to a state of rest.

Investing is what God expects of us. We may start out on assignments, but God is getting us ready for a period of rest. Now my definition of rest may not be yours. It's not a place where you do nothing. Rather it's a place where the resources over which God gave you dominion are truly working for you. When this occurs you are in a position to fully dedicate your time and energy to carrying out God's will in the earth. See, God wants you to prosper more than you do. He wants your God-given resources to work for you because at that point you are operating like Him and *that* is your full potential.

Seeds for Your Soil

God Empowered Man: Genesis 1

1. What blueprint did God use when He created mankind?

2. What did God give mankind authority over?

3. How many types of "man" did God make?

4. For what purpose did God create mankind?

5. How did God feel after He made man?

Man's Responsibility: Genesis 2

1. What did God do after He created mankind?

2. What was the first job that God gave man?

3. What instructions did God give man?

4. Why did God introduce the man to the woman?

5. Why is the husband responsible for his wife?

The Riches of God's Grace: Ephesians 3

1. What do the riches of God provide us with?

2. What size blessing can we expect from God if we do His will?

CHAPTER 3

THE GREATEST INVESTOR THE WORLD HAS EVER KNOWN

What Jesus Christ Taught Mankind about Investing

How Adam Lost a Fortune!

In the book of John we read that not only was the Son present during creation, but He was in fact responsible for making everything. Obviously, the Son had a complete understanding of the process of wealth creation. Man, created in God's image and likeness, had full access to God's creative ability. So as far as creating wealth goes, Adam had the master plan. Now for those who don't know, Adam was the name God used to refer to both man and woman prior to the fall.

> *Gen. 1:27* "So God Created man in His image, in the image of God created He him; male and female created He them."

> *Gen. 5:2* "Male and female created He (God) them; and blessed them, and called their name Adam, in the day when they were created."

These verses tell us that men and women alike have full access to this wealth-generating ability. Man and woman (wombed man), are perfect complements and equals in the eyesight of God. So when men and women work together as God intended, they are a complete force. Some couples are having trouble generating wealth because they don't have a shared purpose or vision. But that's another book, so back to the matter at hand.

There is another character we must introduce as we replay the events leading to the fall. That character is Satan himself. I will not spend much time talking about Satan, because every born again, Spirit-filled believer has power over the enemy and all his works. Nevertheless, we must examine how Satan usurped authority over the first man, so that we can understand how to reclaim a position of authority in our own lives. Authority comes from God. The ability to create wealth comes from God. Satan does not have the power to overthrow man; he only seeks to deceive us so that we disobey God. Only then are we powerless over his devices. Satan also does not have the ability to create; he can only mimic the things of God. This is why the enemy tries to tempt men with things that are temporal and feign ownership of things that actually belong to God. So while we cannot absolve Adam from the well-chronicled fall of man, it will serve us well to recognize the tricks of the enemy.

The Bible tells us that Satan our adversary comes for to steal, kill, and destroy (John 10:10). What does he come to steal, kill, and destroy? He comes to steal and destroy the things that God has given you. He comes to kill your dreams and visions. His goal is to render you useless. How does he do that? It's very simple! He attempts to trick you into separating yourself from God, who is the source of all of your resources and creative abilities. That is what sin does. When the enemy deceived Adam, causing man to sin, we gave up our role as investors and took on the role of servants.

> *Gen. 3:23* "Therefore the Lord God sent him forth from the Garden of Eden, to till the ground from whence he was taken."

Because man was no longer in communion with God, the ultimate authority, they gave up their God-given authority. So one of the primary keys to creating wealth is restoring the relationship with God that mankind enjoyed in the beginning.

It's Not What You Know... It's Who You Know!

Now I am sure that most, if not all, of my readers have heard this phrase before. The basic premise is that having the right relationships (with people) will help an individual in business and/or personal endeavors. This actually mirrors an important spiritual principle. The ability to generate wealth, lead truly productive lives, find real happiness and obtain eternal life is wholly dependent on our relationship with God. This relationship can only be established through His Son Jesus Christ. Christ communicated this important principle to His disciples near the end of His earthly ministry.

> *John 15:4-5* "Abide in me and I in you, as the branch cannot bear fruit of itself, except it abide in the vine; no more can ye except ye abide in me. I am the vine, ye are the branches. He that abideth in me and I in him, the same bringeth forth much fruit: for without me, ye can do nothing."

In essence, true productivity — the ability to produce natural and spiritual fruit — is a direct result of having the proper relationship with God the Father. Remember, your wealth comes as a result of inheritance. When we accept Jesus Christ as our Lord, we become joint heirs with Him (i.e., we also have a claim on the world and everything that's in it). Now receiving an inheritance doesn't mean that we are no longer required to do anything. After all, the Bible tells us that faith without works is dead (James 2:20). However, what this does imply is that once our relationship with God is restored, we have complete access to God's creative ability and spiritual resources. The Holy Spirit is also able to lead us in the full deployment of our gifts, talents, and abilities. And these are the building blocks for generating wealth.

> *Ps. 112:1-3* "Blessed is the man that feareth the Lord (has the right relationship with God), that delighted greatly in His (the Lord's) commandments. His seed shall be mighty upon the earth: the generation of the upright shall be blessed. Wealth and riches shall be in his house: and his righteousness endureth for ever."

> *Mark 8:36-37* "For what shall it profit a man, if he shall gain the whole world, and lose his own soul? Or what shall a man give in exchange for his soul?"

> *John 10:9-10* "I am the door: by me if any man enter in, he shall be saved, and shall go in and out, and find pasture. The thief (Satan) cometh for to steal, kill and to destroy: I am come that they (mankind) might have life, and that they might have it more abundantly."

Jesus came into the world for the express purpose of restoring man as God's authority in the earth. His ultimate goal was to return man to their proper place as investors. Make no mistake! Jesus died to save us from our sins. However, that was not the only reason He came. I'll give you an example to point out the distinction. If my four-month-old son starts crying, I immediately head for his room and begin a battery of checks. Is he wet? Is he hungry? Does he just want attention? My primary objective is to help him stop crying. Once I identify the need, I meet it. However, my ultimate goal is not to stop the crying, but to fully meet his need.

In turn, salvation is one of several objectives in God's redemptive plan. Salvation is often the focus because if Jesus does not cover the sin in our lives, the rest of the process is null and void. However, keep in mind that an objective is not a purpose or goal. The goal represents the finish line or final product. The objectives are merely the steps that get us there. Salvation, justification, consecration, and restoration are all objectives in God's ultimate plan to reestablish man as His authority in the earth. Then with our God-given authority restored, we can become fruitful, multiply, and replenish the earth.

If you really think about it, it makes perfect sense. Why would God deliver an individual, if He didn't plan to utilize that individual's life? He wouldn't! Remember, God is an investor. Like any investor, He fully expects a return on His investment. The passage in the book of John clearly states that Jesus' goal is for you to enjoy an abundant life. So Jesus came not only to give you your life back, but also to ensure that you lead a productive life. Salvation was never part of the original plan, but a necessary step in God's backup plan. In other words, Jesus came to restore God's original plan for man - the plan to be fruitful. This is why Jesus is referred to as the last Adam (1 Cor. 15:45). Jesus did what God's first man failed to do. He led a completely productive life and fulfilled God's purpose for His earthly life.

Jesus had a two primary motives for coming to earth in the form of man. First, He came to make the ultimate sacrifice. It was only through the shedding of innocent blood that we could be reconciled back to the Father. Because a man brought sin into the world, another man would have to be sacrificed to cover sin. His second motive is the one we often overlook. Jesus came to show us the power we possess when we have the right relationship with God. Why do you think He had an earthly ministry? He could have died a perfect sacrifice without preaching one sermon. Why do you think He performed miracles? Some would say to prove He was the Son of God. However, Jesus didn't have an identity crisis — we do! Jesus knew exactly who He was and what He was capable of doing. He performed miracles to convert unbelievers as well as to show us what we are capable of achieving when we're hooked up with God.

> *John 14:12* "Verily, verily, I say unto you, he that believeth on me (Jesus), the works that I do shall he do also; and even greater than these shall he do; because I go unto the father."

Jesus' life demonstrates what a man led by God's Spirit can accomplish. He came to show us how to live abundantly. Think about it. From the time He began His earthly ministry, He never worked a job in the traditional sense. Yet He never lacked or wanted for anything. He had scores of disciples traveling with Him. (It came down to twelve in the latter half of His ministry.) Yet you never read about one of them lacking food or substance. That means that Jesus had enough to go around. Now if that doesn't qualify as abundant living, I don't know what does. Abundant living is what Christ was all about.

What Jesus Taught Concerning Money

If Jesus is our perfect example, it seems only fitting to investigate His attitude toward investing. But as we deal with money, remember that our focus is much bigger. This book is about resources and their proper use.

> *Matt. 6:24* "No man can serve two masters: for either he will hate the one, and love the other; or else he will

hold to the one, and despise the other. Ye cannot serve
God and mammon."

Jesus' point is clear. He never said you couldn't have money. He
said it is impossible to serve both God and money. The word *serve*,
as it is used in this particular verse, comes from the Greek word
douleuo (dool-yoo'-o), which means to enter into bondage. In
other words, acquiring money can't be more important than doing
God's will. If money takes priority over serving God, you will become a slave to your desire for money and the things you can acquire with it. The second epistle to the church at Corinth tells us
that when we have God's Spirit, we have liberty. So if you put God
first, you obtain everlasting life and he'll let you have some money
too. Serving God gives us the right attitude toward money. So instead of serving money, money will serve you. That is what investing is all about.

Now that we have touched on what the scripture *does* say, let's be
clear on what it *doesn't* say. It doesn't say you can't work for money.
It doesn't say you can't spend money. And it certainly doesn't say you
can't invest money. In fact, Jesus teaches just the opposite. Unfortunately, some folks believe Christianity is a poor man's religion. But
God gave the entire world to His Son Jesus Christ. Now as best as I
can tell, that would make Him the richest man that has ever lived.
And guess what? He's alive and well.

The Bible tells us in the book of James that we have not, because
we ask not (James 4:2). Now before you put down the book and go
ask God for some money, let me tell you, it doesn't work that way. I
believe this scripture means to ask *how* not to ask *for*, so it's going to
require some work on your part. Remember Deut. 8:18 tells us that
God gives us the power to get wealth. It doesn't say He just gives us
wealth. There is plenty of money out there if you ask God how to go
about obtaining it.

Do You Recognize a Good Investment When You See It?

In chapter 2 we defined the term *invest* as the act of furnishing with power and authority. This is not the definition that comes to mind when most folks think of the term *invest*, but that's because we are trained to think small. Let's look at it more closely. If you buy a stock, you have turned over both power and authority to another. In particular, you have empowered the management team to make decisions on your behalf and you have given them authority over your resources. In return for your transfer of power and authority, you receive partial ownership in the company. Your stock certificate represents that ownership. However, your proportional claim on the total assets of the company is your actual investment. Now here comes the tough part. There are a lot of potential investments out there. A good steward must be capable identifying good investments.

First things first. Let us establish a working definition for *investment*. An investment is merely what you receive in return for contributing a resource. Furthermore, an investment is expected to provide a future benefit that exceeds the value of the resource that is given in exchange. So when you buy a stock, you exchange cash (a claim on resources) for an investment (partial ownership in a company). You often here people say, "I made an investment of X." They're using the wrong language. They may be referring to money, time, or another resource, but X is not the investment. When you invest $100 to buy stock, that $100 is not your investment. The partial ownership is your investment. The $100 just represents the current value of that investment. You can invest money, but money can never be an investment. You can invest time, but time can never be an investment. This concept is discussed in greater detail in chapter 4.

Now that we have established what an investment is, let us determine how to separate the wheat (good investments) from the tares (bad investments). I have worked in the financial services field for the past seven years and I have six years of business education represented by both a bachelors and a masters degree in accounting/finance. Now that doesn't necessarily amount to a lot, but it's more than nothing. Despite my education and experience, I still have great difficulty identifying good investments. No matter how much research I do, I still produce average performance in my personal stock portfolio. One might conclude that I simply don't have the talent or skill for such an endeavor. However, empirical evidence shows that more than 90 percent of professional money managers underperform the market. In layman's terms that means that the individuals who are paid to invest on behalf of the general public actually have a hard time identifying good investments themselves - and these are the experts!

While professional money managers have a hard time beating the market, their performance is still considerably better than the relatively uninformed individual investor. Just about any financial advisor will tell you that you are better served buying a mutual fund than buying individual stocks. In other words, you are better off outsourcing this difficult task to a professional investor than taking it on yourself. I have come to a somewhat similar conclusion. Initially, I am much better off identifying a good *investor*, as opposed to looking for good *investments*. This is true both naturally and spiritually. If I can partner with a good investor, I have the benefit of receiving good investment advice. But more importantly, I have the opportunity to learn and become a good investor myself. Jesus is the greatest investor the world has ever known. When you partner with Him you have access to all the investing expertise you will ever need. The Holy Spirit, which is the way He manifests Himself in the lives of born-again believers, gives you all the power you need to distinguish good investments from bad investments. I am not suggesting the Holy Spirit will help you pick stocks. However, I am declaring the Holy Spirit will guide you in the allocation of your God-given resources. Remember, money is a claim on resources.

Do You Recognize a Good Investor When You See One?

A good investment for one individual does not necessarily qualify as a good investment for another individual. This is because we have different needs. I cannot define what a *good investment* is for you. This is why it is essential to identify a *good investor*. This allows you to learn the craft of investing. Fortunately, identifying a good investor is straightforward. Every good investor must possess two qualities. They must be able to multiply your resources — provide more than you started with — and add value to your resources — provide a more valuable product than whatever you began with. Jesus is the master of both.

In Matthew 14 we find a perfect example of a true investor. Jesus had ventured out to a desert place where a multitude of people followed Him. Jesus was overcome with compassion for the multitude and spent the entire day healing the sick and ministering. When evening arrived, His disciples suggested that Jesus send the multitude away so they could buy food to eat. Jesus directed the disciples to feed the multitude. Now the multitude consisted of five thousand men — and this did not include women and children (John 14:21). This seemed to be an impossible request to fulfill because the disciples had limited provisions. In fact, the scripture tells us they only had five loaves of bread and two fishes. The issue that Jesus confronted is no different than a major issue we see today: too many consumers and not enough investors. Let's examine how Jesus the investor responds.

> *Matt. 14:19-20* "And He commanded the multitude to sit down on the grass, and He took the five loaves and the two fishes, and looking up to heaven, He blessed and brake, and gave the loaves to His disciples, and the disciples to the multitude. And they did all eat, and were filled: and they took up the fragments that remained twelve baskets full."

The first quality we attributed to an investor was the ability to multiply resources. Jesus took the limited resources that the disciples had and multiplied them such that they were able to feed thousands of people. Not only did the entire multitude eat until they were filled, but the disciples were left with far more resources than they started with.

During the early days of His ministry, Jesus attended a wedding at which His mother Mary was also present. As destiny would have it, the host ran out of wine. Mary informed Jesus that the wine supply had been exhausted in hopes that He would assist. Jesus instructed those present to fill six large water pots with water. After the water pots were filled, He had the servants draw from the water pots and present the drink to the governor of the feast. Jesus not only turned the water into wine, but the governor suggested it was the best portion of wine he was served all day.

> *John 2:9-10* "When the ruler of the feast had tasted the water that was made wine and knew not whence it was: the governor of the feast called the bridegroom, and saith unto him, every man at the beginning doth set forth good wine; and when men have well drunk, then that which is worse: but thou hast kept the good wine until now."

The second quality we attributed to an investor was the ability to add value. Jesus took water, a readily available commodity, which carried little value, and turned it into wine, which was unavailable and thus carried a high value. Jesus didn't provide just any old product. He provided them with the best wine they had been served all day (probably in their whole life). Clearly Jesus provided them with a more valuable product than what they started with.

Jesus' Attitude toward Investing

In chapter 2 we examined God's attitude toward investing. As they say, the proverbial acorn doesn't fall too far from the tree. In Matthew 25, Jesus teaches on the parable of the talents. A *talent* was a sum of money denominated in either gold or silver. The value of the currency was determined by its weight. The Jewish talent contained three thousand shekels and weighed approximately 114 pounds. The Roman-Attic talent, which is likely the one referred to in New Testament scripture, totaled six thousand denarii or drachmas and weighed about 91 pounds. In today's dollars, one talent of gold would be equivalent to nearly half of a million dollars. If you pictured a handful of coins when you read the 25th chapter of Matthew, just one word of advice: expand your mind. Jesus was dealing with big money not small change. We don't serve a small-change God.

> *Matt. 25:15* "For as a man traveling into a far country, called his own servants, and delivered unto them his goods. And unto one he gave five talents, to another two, and to another one; to every man according to his several ability; and straightway took his journey."

The wealthy man in this parable represents God. Now some might conclude that the man was unfair because he did not divide his wealth equally. Wrong answer. (News flash: It was never their money to begin with!) The man was a good steward. He distributed the wealth to the servants based on the gifts they possessed. This is an important lesson because many individuals are discontent with the resources God has provided them. But if you truly understand God's Word, you know that God has given you all the resources you need to enjoy abundant living. We become discontent when we fail to fully utilize our gifts or fail to maximize our potential.

The servant with five talents used his ability (gifts) and produced five additional talents. The servant with two talents used his ability (gifts) and produced two additional talents. But the servant with one talent buried the talent and waited for his lord to return. The first two individuals produced the same return. Each doubled the original investment and provided their lord with a 100 percent return. When you read verses 21 and 23 you find that each man received exactly the same response from their lord.

> *Matthew 25: 21 or 23* "His lord said unto him, Well done, good and faithful servant: thou hast been faithful over a few things, I will make you ruler over many things: enter into the joy of the lord."

Both men received the same reward from the Lord because they maximized their potential. They gave God 100 percent and nothing less. You can also discover an important spiritual principle in this parable. God is never concerned with what you have. He gave it to you in the first place. God is only concerned about what you do with what you have. God also doesn't want you to be concerned with what others have. Notice that the servant with two talents was not distracted by what the other servants had. He was neither high-minded because he had more than the servant with one talent, nor was he discontent because the first servant had five talents. Either of these attitudes cause you to underachieve and fall short of your potential. This servant simply decided to give God 100 percent. God expects the same from every one of us.

Now I'd love to end the story on that high note, but this is only half of the lesson. We must examine the actions of the third servant to fully appreciate the teaching.

> *Matt. 25:25* "And I was afraid, and went and hid thy talent."

The third servant decided to bury the talent he had received from his lord. He withheld the gift that God had given him rather than invest it by fully utilizing his abilities. When his lord returned, the servant made excuses because he could only return that which he started with. Let's read the lord's response to the third servant.

> *Matt. 25:26-28* "Thou wicked and slothful servant, thou knowest that I reap where I sowed not, and gather where I have not strawed: Though oughtest therefore to put my money to the exchangers, and at my coming I should have received mine with usury. Take therefore the talent from him, and give it unto him which hath ten talents."

The lord was angry when he realized that his servant hadn't produced anything with the resources he had given him. He calls the servant wicked and slothful. The term *wicked* in this verse is the Greek word *poneros* (pon-ay-ros'), which means evil or opposed to God's will. The word *slothful* as it is used in this passage simply means sluggish or lazy. This is the same response we can expect from God when we fail to utilize the gifts that He has given us and waste the resources He has supplied. We can take it a step further and rightfully conclude that we are out of the will of God when we fail to invest the resources He has provided us with. The lord tells his servant that he should at least have loaned out the money so that he could have collected usury (that's old school for interest). The Word is telling us that if we don't have productive uses for our resources, we should give them to someone who will do something productive with them. While this course of action falls short of what we are capable of, it demonstrates a reverence for the things of God and an appreciation for what God is doing in the lives of believers. This is why some people are tremendously blessed purely because of their willingness to give to the Church and build God's Kingdom.

There is a subtle but important point in verse 28. The lord declares that the talent should be taken from the unproductive servant. The parable tells us that each of the servants had several abilities, these are the gifts that God gives every one of us. Notice that the lord takes away the talent, the money or resources, and not the abilities. God will never take away the gifts He has given you (Rom. 11:29). However, the Bible also tells us in Eccl. 3:1 that there is a set time to every purpose on earth. In other words, you have a certain allotment of time to accomplish what God has purposed for you to do. The servant in the parable ran out of time so his lord took away his resources. God operates the same way in all of our lives. If we fail to lead productive lives, God will take the resources He set aside for us and give them to someone who will do His will. Simply put, the amount of resources God gives us is directly related to how we allocate the time we have. Much more on this topic in chapter 4.

The lord not only takes the talent from the unproductive servant, but he gives it to the servant with ten talents. He chose this servant according to his ability. This servant had the ability to produce more (in absolute terms) and this is why he was given more resources. We are often distracted by what others have, failing to recognize that those resources may just be a function of God's calling on their lives. They have greater resources, because they have a greater need for resources. It has nothing to do with the importance of their calling or purpose. God is only concerned that we fulfill our purpose, whatever it may be. As long as we finish our own personal course, our reward is in heaven.

> *2 Tim. 4:7* "I have fought the good fight, I have finished my course, I have kept the faith: Hence forth there is laid up for me a crown of righteousness, which the Lord, the righteous judge, shall give me at that day, and not to me only, but unto all them that love His appearing."

The Poverty Problem

The conclusion of the parable has some important lessons for believers and society as a whole. Let us read the conclusion of the matter and observe how the lord rewards the servant whom he is displeased with.

> *Matt. 25:29-30* "For unto every one that hath shall be given, but from him that hath not shall be taken away even that which he hath. And cast ye the unprofitable servant into outer darkness: there shall be weeping and gnashing of teeth."

I believe this scripture addresses one of the more troubling problems the world faces. This is the issue of poverty. Despite the vast wealth in the world, a large percentage of the world's population languishes in poverty. I want to make a bold statement here. Poverty is not a condition (as men like to define it), it is a choice. I know some people will take exception to my conclusion, but hear me out. No one chooses to be poor. However, everyone who continues in poverty has made a choice to remain poor. The reason we have not solved the poverty problem is that we have relied on man's system and not God's system. Man's system is designed to provide necessities for those in need. The problem lies in the fact that another man can *never* meet your needs — only God and God alone.

Phil. 4:19 says, "But my God shall supply all your need according to His riches and glory by Christ Jesus." God doesn't supply our needs the way man does, by giving us handouts. God reveals to us our gifts and our purpose. As you utilize your gifts and seek to fulfill your purpose, God provides for all of your needs. That is why Prov. 18:16 states that a man's gift maketh room for him. The word *room* in this context means opportunity or provision. Bluntly put, God only provides for you if you are productive. Paul goes as far as to state in his second epistle to the Thessalonians that if any would not work, then they shouldn't be allowed to eat (2 Thess. 3:10). The sad fact is that the systems we have put in place to address poverty have taught people to be unproductive and shifted their dependence from God to man.

The situation is even more grave than you may think. When we think *poor*, we think *destitute*, but this is not how God thinks. If you consult the dictionary for the definition of *poor*, you will find the term *unproductive*. Anyone who is unproductive is poor in God's eyesight. This is why Matt. 25:29 declares, "For unto every one that hath shall be given, but from him that hath not should be taken away even that which he hath." If you are unproductive, you will lose what you have. It's just that simple.

The Word declares that the unprofitable servant should be cast into "outer darkness," otherwise known as hell. So you see, God is all about productivity. God wants us to live a life of abundance and has given us all the resources we need to accomplish this. When we choose to be productive, we choose life — eternity with God, and not death — separation from God. Productivity is the essence of life. We even refer to birth as reproduction. When God gave man life, He defined man's existence by commanding man to be productive. I don't know about you, but I choose life.

Seeds for Your Soil

Bearing Good Fruit: John 15

1. How does God respond when we invest wisely?

2. What is the key ingredient to successful investing?

3. Do godly investments stand the test of time?

The Value of Salvation: Mark 8:34-38

1. What does salvation cost?

2. How much is salvation worth?

Heavenly Investments: Matt. 6:19-24

1. What should be the focus of investing?

2. What should our attitude be toward investing?

3. What priority should our personal investments take?

Jesus the Quintessential Investor: Matt. 14:15-21

1. What did Jesus do when He saw others in need?

2. What did Jesus do with the resources at His disposal?

Investing Wisely: Matt. 25:14-30

1. Does God give us all the same amount of resources?

2. What does God expect us to do with the resources we are given?

3. How does God respond when we invest our resources wisely?

4. How does God respond when we fail to invest our resources wisely?

PART II

Principles of Investing

CHAPTER 4

GETTING YOUR RESOURCES TO WORK FOR YOU

Spiritual Insight into Resource Allocation

The Resource You Can't Live Without

What's the most important resource that God gave man, after the fall? Time is up! Or shall I say *time* is it. Satan thought he had everything figured out. He had deceived man, causing them to disobey God. Their sin or disobedience resulted in separation from God. Anything that is separated from God is dead or unproductive. Furthermore, the introduction of sin caused the whole world to lose God's divine order. And just when it appeared as though Adam had their final curtain call, God did one of those things only God can do.

> *Gen. 3:17* "Because thou hast hearkened unto the voice of thy wife and hast eaten of the tree, of which I commanded thee, saying Thou shalt not eat of it: cursed is the ground for thy sake (instead of you); in sorrow shalt thou eat of it all the days of thy life (days numbered or time instituted)."

Instead of cursing man, God cursed the ground. (A price had to be paid for sin.) God then numbered the days of man's life. Before sin, man lived in eternity with God. For years, I read this scripture and felt sorry for Adam and all humanity. But then I realized that God had flipped the script. Man should have been done away with on the spot. After all, we disobeyed God. But God, in the midst of chastising man, gave us a resource that we could not live without. That resource is time. Without time, there would have been no redemptive plan. There would have been no Jesus Christ and there would have been no salvation. God needed time to save His man. And man needed time to be restored by God. God, who is everlasting, split eternity down the middle and instituted time. Time is a resource instituted specifically for man. That's how special we are to God. The Bible tells us that a thousand years are like one day to God. Clearly God has no need for time, but we need all the time we can get!

Time Waits for No Man

Is time really our most valuable resource? In order to answer this question we must begin by establishing a working definition for the term *resource*. In *Stop Digging!* Brother Goins defines a resource as the entire means available for the purpose of productivity or maturity. Let's consider another possible definition. A resource can also be defined as a deposit used for supply or support. Resources come in many forms. There are natural resources, such as water, minerals, and fuels. There are spiritual resources, such as the Holy Spirit. Books, records, the internet, and other people are also resources. Every resource in the earth was provided to support man.

Let's break down the word *resource*. The root word is *source*, which means origin. By definition every resource originates from God. The prefix *re* means to go back. It precedes the root word *source*, because a resource is designed to take you back to the origin or the originator. In other words, the productive use of any resource

48

brings you in line with God's will or closer to God. God is the source of everything you need. So when you expend the natural or spiritual deposits God has provided you with, God *re-sources* you — He provides you with more resources. Notice I used the word *expend* and not the word *spend*. To expend means to utilize, whereas to spend means to consume or exhaust. Therefore a business investment is referred to as an expenditure.

Now, back to time. Think of any productive task in your life. Praying, reading a book, working to support your family, working out at the gym, preparing a meal — there is an endless list of productive tasks. These tasks all require varied resources, but there is one that is common to all. Time! Time is a necessary component of *everything* we do. Thinking is something we do without even moving a muscle. Assuming you're in your right mind (the mind of Christ), thinking is very productive. Yet even thinking requires an investment of time.

Unlike people, time is always moving. In fact, time is always moving toward God. God designed time that way to encourage us to move in the same direction. See, God doesn't make you move. He just keeps the clock of life moving so that you have to keep up with it. Eventually mankind will run out of time (i.e., time will outrun some of mankind), and we will have to account for the way we utilized this essential resource. Productivity, which is the proper use of time, allows you to keep up with time. Time is on its way back to God, returning to its source. But if you are unproductive, time simply passes you by.

Feel Like You Are Having a Devil of a Time?

Here's a revelation for you. The devil hates time. I mean, he really hates time. Think about it. God gave you plenty of it and didn't give him any. He messed up. Eternal damnation! You messed up. Give 'em a little time God says. And you think God doesn't play favorites.

Satan is burning mad that God gave us a second chance — after all, that's what time is — and God gave him a one-way ticket to the lake a fire — hell is just a layover. To really get an understanding of why Satan is opposed to time, let's go back to the fall of man.

> *Gen. 3:14-15* "And the Lord God said unto the serpent (the embodiment of Satan), Because thou hast done this (deceived the woman), thou art cursed above all cattle, and above every beast of the field; upon thy belly shalt thy go, and dust shalt thou eat all the days of thy life: And I will pit enmity between thee and the woman, and between thy seed (workers of iniquity) and her seed (Jesus, the body of Christ); it shall bruise thy head, and thou shalt bruise His heel"

God not only cursed the serpent, but He designed the system so that time would work against Satan. He sentenced the serpent to go on his belly for all of time. In other words, Satan was abased and was decreed by God to be no match for the Spirit-filled man. Now I want you to get this next point, because it is deep. Time is Satan's curse. While time brings man closer to God, it only pushes Satan further away from God. Surely there is no greater curse than that. It is like being stranded on death row with no hope for an appeal. As he awaits the execution of his sentence, he must helplessly watch God redeem man.

Are You Winning the Time Battle?

Did you know that Satan your adversary has waged war on time? Time has all the value in the world to you, and no value at all to him. When Satan turned against God he was condemned for all eternity. He has been judged and is merely waiting for his sentence to be carried out. Satan's sentence is irrevocable — he has no second chance.

Satan's sole objective is to cause man, God's prized possession, to share the same fate. Trust me, this has everything to do with investing. Time is a necessary component of everything we do. In other words, time gives value to everything we do. If you sow a seed, you need time for it to grow. If you mix cement, you need time for it to set. And if you make an investment, you need time for it to yield a return. That is why Satan has waged war on time.

> *1 Pet. 5:6-8* "Humble yourselves therefore under the mighty hand of God, that He may exalt you in due time: Casting all your care upon Him; for He careth for you. Be sober, be vigilant; because your adversary the devil, as a roaring lion, walketh about, seeking whom he may devour:"

Satan is restricted from touching any man except when God allows it. That is why the scripture reads "seeking whom he *may* devour." Satan attempts to lead us into situations in which time works against us. I believe this is why there are so many distractions in the world today. It is a concerted effort by the enemy to get us to waste time. Just look around your home. Many of us have a television or stereo in every room. Not to mention the video games. Pure and simple, this is the enemy at work. That is why the scripture describes him as a lion. For all the fuss about the lion's dominance, it is his cunning that is his true strength. The lion seeks out the prey that is injured or unhealthy — the ones overtaken by sin. He also seeks those who have strayed from the fold — those who lack discipline. The lion carefully selects his prey, and patiently waits for just the right moment. It is at the unsuspecting victim's most vulnerable state that he goes in for the kill. See, the enemy doesn't necessarily seek to devour your body; he actually seeks to devour your time.

What Is Time Worth to You?

Since time is a necessary component for everything we do in the natural world, time is the ingredient that establishes value. Think about it. You are compensated on your job as a result of the *time* you spend working there. Relationships with friends and family are valuable because you spend *time* with these individuals. Precious minerals, resources and gems only have value because of the *time* they spent buried deep in the earth. In the natural realm, nothing has value without time. If you were given a billion dollars and passed away the next moment, the money would have absolutely no value to you. Just about everything that God has called us to do requires two inputs: time and money. Let's examine how these two inputs work together.

First, back to the basics. Money is a medium of exchange. It can be looked at as a resource, but more accurately it is a claim on resources (i.e., money represents resources you will utilize in the future). Time is our most important resource. People often say that money can't buy you love. It also can't buy you time — both are gifts from God. God gave man time for the express purpose of carrying out His will in the earth. Anything short of carrying out God's will is a waste of time.

> *Eccl. 9:11-12* "I returned, and saw under the sun, that the race is not given to the swift, nor the battle to the strong, neither yet bread to the wise, nor yet riches to men of understanding, nor yet favour to men of skill; but time and chance (both controlled by God) happeneth to them all. For man also knoweth not his time: as the fishes that are taken in an evil net, and the birds that are caught in the snare; so are the sons of men snared in an evil time, when it falleth suddenly upon them."

This scripture tells us the value of time. The Word says that regardless of an individual's stature — position, skill, and wealth — or understanding — knowledge and wisdom — that individual cannot control time or chance. The scripture states that they both just happen, or, in other words, God controls both time and chance. Many individuals have concluded that good things happen by chance, but with God, good things happen by design. And while none of us know precisely how much time we will be here, God knew exactly how much time to give us when He sent us here. If we don't appropriately value our time, we are like the fishes taken in an evil net — time falls upon us suddenly. Those who don't value time are enslaved to the things of this world — work, money, television, unhealthy relationships, or any number of things. Inappropriate amounts of time spent on these things become evil. God is the only one who knows how much time each one of us is allotted. If we truly value time, we will develop our relationship with Him.

It's about Time You Went to Work

Do you feel as though you are stuck on your present job? Do you feel like your employer doesn't appreciate you? Do you feel as though you are underpaid? When you are on your job, would you rather be somewhere else? When you are on your job, do you feel frustrated or unfulfilled? If you answered yes to any or all of these questions, I suspect your job may not be the best use of your time. I'll also let you in on a secret. Until you go to work for God, you will never shake those feelings. Let's revisit our friend Adam and see if he can help us understand why.

We concluded in chapter 2 that God designated Adam as His investor here on earth. But before God allowed Adam to pursue his life's work as an investor, He gave him a job — to dress and keep the garden. Adam's job served a dual purpose. It provided him with a sense of responsibility and it caused him to realize his gifts, talents, and abilities. While the job certainly had its perks — great location, a beautiful co-worker, and pretty good hours — it was never intended to take the place of his work. God's long-range plan was to have Adam spend eternity fulfilling his purpose. Adam's severed relationship with God caused Adam to get stuck on the job. Like Adam, many of us find ourselves stuck on a job. God gave Adam time to get back on track and discover his life's work. In doing so, God did the same for every one of us. Problem is, most folks invest all of their time in their job and have nothing left to invest in their work. While your job can help you discover your gifts, talents, and abilities, only your work allows you to fully deploy them. And only your work allows you to make full productive use of time.

God had big plans for Adam, but he shirked responsibility and God could not promote him to his purpose. Like Adam, God has big plans for you. But for many of us, our jobs are our biggest waste of time. I know, you are vice president of such and such or assistant manager of this and that. But odds are that you're wasting time. See, God knew we would have trouble developing the appropriate perspective of our jobs. After all, the first man got stuck on his job. So God decided to drop a little knowledge in the book of Ecclesiastes to help us put our jobs into the proper perspective.

> *Eccl. 3:9-11* "What profit hath he that worketh in that wherein he laboreth? (What good is having a job if you are not fulfilling your purpose?) I have seen travail (I have seen people struggle and/or I have seen people who are miserable), which God hath given the sons of men to be exercised in it (yet God has given us the ability to profit from our work). He hath made everything beautiful (at its best or just right) in His time (with the appropriate investment of time):"

Have you ever noticed how God's plan for us is so much better than the one we devise ourselves? In this passage of scripture, God reveals to us that having a job is not enough. Fulfilling our purpose is where the real profit is. Sadly, many well-intentioned, short-sighted individuals have steered others into jobs and careers that don't complement God's plan for their lives. As a result, many people are unhappy and struggle day-to-day because they are doing something they weren't designed to do. It's as if time is fighting against them.

Just do the math. We spend most of our waking hours either on our job, commuting to and from our job, or preparing for our job. Even if you work a standard 9 to 5 — and most folks don't these days — you likely dedicate about 50 hours per week to your job. Individuals in service-oriented professions such as business, medicine, or law, dedicate 60, 80 even 100 hours per week to their profession. Since the average individual is physically awake 110 to 125 hours per week, the dilemma is clear. With such demands on our time, it is essential that our job accommodate God's plan for our life and not the other way around. After all, how else can we truly invest in our personal development, our relationships with loved ones, and our relationship with God?

I am not suggesting that you run out and quit your job. However, I would suggest that you seek God to determine if your job lines up with His will for your life. The right job is not merely a function of the time commitment. Some individuals can punch the clock for 80 hours per week and still manage to do a great work for God. Others don't have the same grace and can barely manage 40. Allow God to reveal to you the appropriate time commitment. I believe some people are fortunate enough to find the perfect job, but not perfect in the way we like to think. *Perfect*, as it is used in the Bible, often means complete. So some individuals find jobs that are in line with God's direction for their lives, and the job perfects them.

Most of us will have to settle for a good job — one God approves of. In my opinion, there is no such thing as the right job — at least not the way we like to think. There are lots of jobs that may be right for you. As long as the one you choose allows you to do your life's work (God's will), take care of yourself (develop), and take care of your family (this includes the church), you have found the right kind of job. If your job causes you to fail in any of these areas, it is the wrong job. Case closed. A good job will allow you to appropriately invest your time and do a great work for God. I'll take the great work, good job combo any day.

My message here is simple. Your job should be a blessing to you and not a burden. It is a resource, and like any other resource, it should help you to accomplish God's purpose for your life. Your job should support your work, not take its place. If all of us are called to be investors, it seems to me that our jobs should provide the means for us to invest. Let's get real. We have jobs because we need money. And if we want to invest — and I'm not just talking about the stock market — we need some money. Here's the catch. The money doesn't matter if you don't have enough time.

If You've Got the Money, God's Got the Time
You may be thinking we've expended a disproportionate amount of time talking about time. Well we did... and we needed to. Time gives value to everything we do in the natural — that includes investing. Any elementary finance text generally begins by teaching the most essential principle of investing. This investing principle is simply known as the *time value of money*. That phrase is a revelation in and of itself. It tells you that money has no value without time. God set up the system so that the two work together, and time is the more essential of the two. The *time value of money*, in essence means that a dollar today is not worth a dollar in the future. If we invest, our dollar is worth substantially more in the future. How-

56

ever, if we simply hold on to it, like the servant with the talent, it is worth substantially less. It's just that simple.

Here's an example. If I give you one dollar today and you stick it in a coffee can and leave it for ten years, it will no longer be worth a dollar. It will still have a nominal or stated value of one dollar, but its real value will be less than a dollar. In ten years that dollar won't enable you to buy the same amount of stuff you can buy with it today. Inflation has averaged about 3 percent or so over the last ten years. If inflation remains constant, the dollar in the coffee can will be worth about 74 cents in ten years. Not only does it fail to gain value, it actually loses value. So what happens if we invest that dollar? If you invest the dollar and receive a 10 percent nominal return (7 percent including the negative effect of the 3 percent inflation), it will be worth about $1.97 at the end of ten years. You have essentially doubled your money, despite that pesky inflation. So by applying the principles of investing, which are God's principles that man borrowed, in ten years time you will be able to afford double what you can afford today (bigger house, bigger car, bigger bank account). If you fail to invest, then in ten years time, you will only be able to afford 75 percent of what you can afford today (smaller house, smaller car, smaller bank account). The math should convince you. It also gives new meaning to the expression "the rich get richer." Investing is just one of the ways in which they do it.

If you're like me, that bigger house, bigger car, bigger bank account line probably got your attention. But before you run out and put all your money in the market, let's make sure our bases are covered. In the first book of this two-part series, Brother Goins laid out the path to becoming a good steward. Good stewardship is what prepares you to be an investor. So if you're not a good steward, you cannot afford to invest. Pure and simple. Many of my family members, friends, and colleagues have asked me for simple investment advice. I always begin with the same inquiry. What's your financial position?

If you have bad credit, are behind on all of your bills, and find yourself buried beneath a mountain of debt, you cannot afford to invest. I generally offer some tips on addressing these issues, but now I can reference Brother Goins for a thorough exposition. A sound financial position is essential for investing because investing is going to cost you something.

The Cost of Investing

I doubt *cost* is the first word that comes to mind when you think about investing. Interestingly enough, cost should be your foremost consideration. The dictionary defines *cost* as the amount paid for something or the loss or penalty incurred in gaining something. In the world of investing, both of these definitions come into play. There is the cost an individual must pay for an individual investment or portfolio of investments. And then there are the individual losses one must endure to receive a portfolio return. Please note that sustaining losses is a normal part of the investment process. Show me an investor who never lost anything and I will show you an investor who never made any money. Show me an investment that doesn't cost anything, and I will show you a fraud or a scheme. Jesus was the greatest investor and to get the abundant return He was seeking, the Bible tells me that it cost Him His life. Many individuals struggle with investments because they have overlooked the essential step of adding up the cost. Let's examine what the Word has to say about this issue.

> *Luke 14:27-30* "And whosoever doth not bear his cross, and come after me, cannot be my disciple. For which of you intending to build a tower, sitteth not down first, and counteth the cost, whether he have to finish. Lest haply, after he hath laid the foundation, and is not able to finish, all that behold begin to mock him,

Saying, this man began to build, and was not able to finish."

Jesus didn't mince words with His disciples. He told them that to become like Him, they would have to give up their lives. In other words, everything that was important to them had to take a back seat to serving God. He goes on to give an example of a man building a tower. The word *tower* in this verse is the Greek word *purgos* (poor'-gos), which refers to a watchtower in a vineyard. A vineyard was a material source of wealth and represented a significant investment of resources. Jesus noted that no investor would set out to build a watchtower, and in turn a vineyard, without considering the total resources required. Failure to carefully consider the costs associated with an investment results in a misappropriation of resources — or an inability to finish. That is failure: the inability to finish. A failed investment is one that does not produce fruit. Without a watchtower, thieves or predators would likely spoil the vineyard and ruin the investment. Careful consideration of costs helps to insure both the safety and the maturity of any investment.

> *Matt. 10:38-39* "And he that taketh not his cross, and followeth after me, is not worthy of me (Christ). He that findeth his life shall lose it: and he that loseth his life for my (Christ's) sake shall find it."

Jesus lets us know that if we are unwilling to follow His example and give our lives over to building God's Kingdom, we are not worthy of the title of investor. "He that findeth his life shall lose it" means that those who use all their time and resources to fulfill selfish desires will lose everything they have in the end. It goes on to say that "he that loseth his life for Christ's sake shall find it." This means if we invest our time and resources toward building God's Kingdom we will gain everlasting life. If you are doing the math, that's a life in return for a life. In numeric terms, that's a 100 percent return. In the first scenario you lose everything. That's a loss of 100 percent. I'm pretty sure that qualifies as a bad investment.

Whether it's stocks, bonds, real estate, or an entrepreneurial venture, there are costs associated with every investment. If we define *cost* as something we give up in exchange for the opportunity to obtain a profit, then the cost is simply what we are willing to sacrifice for an investment. Sound investment strategy begins with a complete and thorough assessment of cost. An astute investor will always establish three things.

1. What is the investment worth? (What price am I willing to pay?)
2. How much can I afford to lose? (Never invest resources that you cannot afford to do without.)
3. Does the potential reward outweigh the expected cost? (The return must cover both the price and any expected losses.)

This three-step process will enable you to make wise use of your resources and build a portfolio that will yield an abundant return.

Seeds for Your Soil

The Result of Sin: Genesis 3

1. What behaviors accompany sin?

2. What is God's response to sin?

3. What is the burden of sin?

Time and Chance: Ecclesiastes 9

1. Can we control life's circumstances?

2. What happens if we fail to trust God during trying times?

The Cost of Investing: Luke 14:26-35

1. What is the cost of discipleship?

2. What happens when we fail to consider the cost of investing?

CHAPTER 5

God's Golden Rules of Investing

Three Keys to Wealth Creation

Everything I Needed to Know about Investing, I Found in the Bible!

I have heard it said that an expert must master a great many things, yet the common man need only master a few. John Train, author of *The Craft of Investing*, begins his book with this very premise. This premise is both simple and paramount. It implies that successful investing is not born from scouring inexhaustible texts devoted to the subject, nor does it result from one's ability to master numerous investment strategies. Successful investing merely results from the mastery of a few key principles. Proper and consistent application of these principles will produce abundant natural and spiritual fruit. Moreover, the application of these principles will restore believers to a position of prominence and prosperity. With our foundation of resource allocation firmly set, let us now search the scriptures and identify these golden rules of investing.

First Things First!

In chapter 3 I concluded that poverty was not a condition, but a choice. When an individual fails to identify and deploy their God-given abilities, they are in essence choosing to become or remain poor. I now turn my attention to another problem that is just as troubling, but even more prevalent. Cliff defined this problem as the digger mentality. It essentially describes those who live from paycheck to paycheck. When I was growing up, we had one descriptive word for this type of individual: broke! While I say this in jest, the harsh reality is that most born-again believers, and most people in general, struggle financially. Their lives are a stark contrast to the abundant life God has declared that believers have a right to. Although Cliff deals with this issue thoroughly in book one, I will briefly examine the cause of the problem to reveal our first investing principle. Matthew 6 deals with several pertinent issues. One of the most critical involves establishing the proper attitude towards material things.

> *Matt. 6:33* "But seek ye first the kingdom of God, and His righteousness (His will); and all these things (material provisions and/or possessions) shall be added unto you."

The key word in this verse is *first*. In the original text it is the Greek word *proton* (pro'-ton), which simply means before or signifies priority. The beginning of the verse could be interpreted like this: "Before you take a course of action, make sure it is in line with God's will." Notice that the scripture doesn't state that you cannot seek material things. However, it does clearly instruct us to seek the kingdom of God and His righteousness. In other words, we should desire to conform to God's image and likeness and we should put His will ahead of our own. In book one, Brother Cliff points out that abundance is a by-product of putting God first. We should begin every day with a resolve to accomplish God's will. In doing so, God will supply both our natural and spiritual needs.

Now the scripture clearly instructs us to seek God first. And therein lies the problem. Financial hardship or struggle is most often the result of failing to seek God first in this critical area of our lives. Look at nature. There is a natural order to things. When something upsets that order, havoc is wreaked on the environment. Spiritual things work in the same manner. If we fail to make God the priority in our lives, we disrupt the order He has established. So if the pursuit of riches and material things is our principal concern, our thoughts and our lives are out of order. As a result, the enemy is empowered to wreak havoc in our finances and destroy our investments. Many individuals are saddled with bad investments because they refused to seek God by studying the word and prayer concerning potential investments. Remember, God is Alpha and Omega. Who better to consult than the one who knows the result of every investment decision we will ever make.

Stop Thief!

Mal. 3:8-10 "Will a man rob God? Yet ye robbed me. But ye say, Wherein have we robbed thee? In tithes and offerings. Ye are cursed with a curse: for ye have robbed me, even this whole nation. Bring me all the tithes into the storehouse, that there may be meat in mine house, and prove me now herewith saith the Lord of hosts, if I will not pour you out a blessing, that there shall not be room enough to receive it."

The scripture asks a very straightforward question. "Will a man rob God?" The word *rob* used in this verse means to steal or deprive of.

The scripture goes on to state that indeed many individuals have chosen to steal from God. Now they say crime doesn't pay. Surely stealing from God has to be the worst kind of theft. God states here that people are robbing Him of tithes and offerings. Tithes are the 10 percent of your substance that you are required to sow into the Church. Offerings are any amount above that which God lays on your heart to give. While this does refer to money, it is much more than that. God clearly expects you to give money, but more importantly He requires you to give of your time.

This may hurt some feelings here, but the primary reason many individuals are in financial distress or saddled with bad investments is because they are stealing from God. For some it is a transgression of omission, for others one of commission. Either way their disobedience to the Word of God has rendered them ineffective as an investor. Again, the earlier scripture told us to make God a priority. This means that He is entitled to the first share of our money and the first share of our time. The scripture states plainly that those who chose to rob God are cursed. This is why they struggle financially and their investments don't bear fruit. However, the scripture also tells us how we can avoid this curse.

Pay God First — God's First Golden Rule

The scripture instructs us to bring all the tithes into the storehouse so that there will be meat in God's house. God is essentially saying that we are required to give God a portion of both our time and our money. By now you understand that time and money belong to God. He has merely afforded us the use of them. For God to carry out His purpose, in the earth He needs meat, provisions available in His house, which is the Church. By giving a portion of things that God has so richly afforded us, we are in fact making Him a priority in our lives.

Now, here comes the revelation. God doesn't need your money.

You only have it because He gave it to you. And if He really wanted it, I suppose He is God enough to take it. God merely set up the system of tithing in order to bless you. Yes, to bless you! The final part of the scripture tells us to try God's advice and see if He won't pour out a blessing that there won't be room enough to receive. God is instructing you to invest. God established the Church as His vehicle to work in the earth. So when God wants to bless you, He does it through the Church. The Church is not a building, rather it is a group of believers that make up the Body of Christ.

When you invest time and money in the Church, God rewards you by pouring out blessings that cannot be measured. These blessings are not monetary in nature, but are spiritual blessings, such as God's favour upon your life. When you give tithes and offerings, you are investing in God's Kingdom and investing in your future. Moreover, this represents God's first golden rule of investing: Pay God first. This principle is similar to one you read in most investment texts that encourage investors to pay themselves first. While it is vitally important that you make investments for yourself and your family before spending your earnings frivolously, nothing should take priority over sowing into God's Kingdom. God is able to do exceeding abundantly above all that we can ask or think (Eph. 3:20). When we choose to invest with God, the returns exceed all we can expect or think. That's what I call compounded returns!

All That Glitters Isn't Gold!

In chapter 4 we established that there is a cost associated with investing. Part of the cost is simply the price of the investment. However, there is a second component of cost. We concluded that there are losses incurred in the process of investing. These losses are a normal part of investing and represent what we give up in exchange for an investment gain. One of the lessons I learned early in my finance career is that minimizing losses is just as important as maximizing gains. Investors not only have to be skilled in identifying profitable investments, they must possess the wisdom to avoid or abandon unprofitable investments. We observed this in chapter 3 as we discussed the parable of the three servants. Their lord was quick to abandon the servant who proved to be a poor steward. He understood how to cut or minimize his losses. If resources go unutilized, this is indeed a loss. While God is faithful to reward us when we sow into His kingdom, we must still endeavor to be led by His Spirit to discern between profitable and unprofitable investments.

> *2 Tim. 2:20* "But in a great house there are not only vessels of gold and of silver, but also of wood and of earth; and some to honour, and some to dishonour."

This is a letter of exhortation from Paul to Timothy. He explains to Timothy that even in a wealthy home there are both fine vessels of great worth and common vessels of little value. Investments are similar. There are some investments that prove to be valuable and some that prove to have little value at all. The difficulty comes in assessing the potential value of the investments. The vessels referred to in this verse have similar and likely identical uses. The difference in value is a function of the composition of the investment and not its use. For example, I can invest an identical amount in two different mutual funds toward my child's education. Each fund has the same intended purpose or use. One fund may appreciate materially, yielding a substantial return, while the other may depreciate substantially, resulting in significant losses. The results are not a component of intended use or initial investment. Both funds were subject to the same time horizon and same market conditions. The difference in results, and subsequently the difference in value, is directly related to the quality of the funds.

Clearly there are distinctions in both the value and appearance of vessels made of precious metals and vessels made of wood or clay. However, in the world of investments the lines become blurred. This is true both naturally and spiritually. There are many people who give the appearance of being Christians, yet turn out to be wolves in sheep's clothing. Likewise, there are many investments that appear desirable, yet in the end, they turn out to be unprofitable and yield little value. The adage is true. All that glitters isn't gold. Fortunately, the Bible gives us clear instruction on how to judge both character and investments.

> *Matt. 7:15-19* "Beware of false prophets which come to you in sheep's clothing, but inwardly are ravening wolves. Ye shall know them by their fruits. Do men gather grapes of thorns, or figs of thistles? Even so every good tree bringeth forth good fruit; but a corrupt tree bringeth forth evil fruit. A good tree cannot bring forth evil fruit, neither can a good tree bring forth good fruit. Every tree that bringeth not forth good fruit is hewn down, and cast into the fire."

The Word of God instructs us to focus on an investment's ability to generate a return, rather than its appearance. Any good investment text will warn you that past investment results are not necessarily a predictor of future performance. This is important to keep in mind. Nevertheless, I would stress to any investor the importance of identifying investors or investments with proven track records. I choose to invest in the things of God because of His proven track record. He promised in His Word that He would never leave me or forsake me (Heb. 13:5). Guess what? He never has.

Now in the natural, things are not as certain as God. However, we can improve the chances of sowing into profitable investments if we examine and compare past results. This is not to say that we are solely limited to investments that have yielded fruit in the past. However, it does suggest that we should be weary of investments that have yet to yield fruit. In most cases it is prudent to avoid investments with poor track records. While this advice may seem strict, the Word clearly tells us that every tree that does not bring forth good fruit is hewn down. Likewise every poor investment will almost surely result in substantial loss, whether natural or spiritual.

A Lesson in Risk Management

I'd love to tell you that choosing an investment with a proven track record is all there is to investing. Unfortunately, it is a bit more challenging. In the natural world, all investments have some degree of risk. Weeding out investments with a history of poor performance is merely a first step. Even investments with a history of strong performance can turn sour. There are also countless potential investments that don't have any track record at all. Finally, market conditions, which is a factor outside of our control, may negatively impact all of the investments we own. Therefore we must develop an investment strategy to best manage these risks. Better yet, we must build a portfolio of investments that takes advantage of these risks.

> *Eccl. 9:11-12* "I returned, and saw under the sun, that the race is not given to the swift, nor the battle to the strong, neither yet bread to the wise, nor yet riches to men of understanding, nor yet favour to men of skill; but time and chance (both controlled by God) happeneth to them all."

This scripture lets us know that certain occurrences or circumstances are out of our control. This mirrors market conditions. So whether you invest in bonds, equities, commodities, art, or real estate, market conditions are largely outside of your control. Certain occurrences, such as recessions, wars, or natural disasters, can negatively impact the market and, therefore, the whole universe of investments. At first blush this may seem like a worrisome form of risk. However, I am going to offer some unconventional advice. As Spirit-filled investors, we needn't concern ourselves with this form of risk because it is totally outside of our control. And anything totally outside of our control is totally controlled by God.

These unforeseen and often unavoidable conditions are referred to in finance as market or systematic risk. In short, it comes with the territory. In the study of finance, we learn that investment returns are always susceptible to market risk. Finance theory helps us to understand both the nature and affect of market risk. The return on a given investment is largely a function of market risk. Consequently, the return merely represents payment for taking on market risk. Interestingly enough, market risk is a valuable form of risk. This is because God controls it. Faith allows you to take advantage of market risk. Chapter 9 explores this topic in greater depth.

There is also unique or unsystematic risk. In a portfolio of investments, some of the things you own will yield losses and others will yield gains, depending on factors unique to each investment. In short, the quality of the individual investment determines whether it produces losses or gains. In essence, unique risk is wholly a function of the choices you make. As investing goes, you are potentially your own worst enemy. Your decisions will make or break you. It is no wonder that unique risk is the form of risk that is most detrimental to portfolio returns in the long run. It is also no wonder that portfolio theory focuses principally on minimizing unique risk.

The Portfolio Approach

The dictionary definition for *unique* is simply being the only one. It logically follows that your unique risk is greatest when you have only one investment. Now, there is nothing wrong with being unique. God tells us that we are fearfully and wonderfully made. However, in God's system our potential is maximized when we work together. Let's examine one of the early decisions God made concerning man.

> *Gen. 2:18* "And the Lord God said, It is not good that man should be alone (all one); I will make a help meet for him."

Remember, man was the most important investment God made in the earth. Man had everything he needed to accomplish God's plan. However, as God analyzed His portfolio, He determined that it was not good for man to be alone or all one. God knew that man would need help. That is why He created a helpmeet — a complimentary investment to balance out His portfolio. There are times when we are down and we need that loved one or friend to assist us or lift our spirit. Investments work the same way. There will be times when one investment in your portfolio loses value. However, other investment gains can offset that loss or overcome it. This is the portfolio approach to investing.

Diversify Your Investments — God's Second Golden Rule

Since unique risk is greatest when you have only one investment, it is logical that increasing the number of investments you own reduces your risk. This is precisely what finance theory teaches us. Adding securities to your portfolio is a process known as diversification. Research has shown that diversification substantially reduces unique risk. In equities, a portfolio of twenty or more stocks has been proven to have a negligible or insignificant amount of unique risk; such a portfolio is considered well diversified. So, while diversification is important, there is no need to go overboard. A reasonable amount of diversification is more than sufficient. Now that we know what finance texts have to say about diversification, let's see what the good book has to say.

> *1 Cor. 12:4-7* "Now there are diversities of gifts, but the same Spirit. And there are differences of administrations, but the same Lord. And there are diversities of operations, but the same God which worketh all in all. But the manifestation of the Spirit is given to every man to profit withal."

In the New Testament we find that God applies the similar principles with respect to investing. In this particular passage, Paul is writing to the church at Corinth concerning spiritual gifts. Paul notes that there is a diversity of gifts that operate in the Body of Christ. Paul lets believers know that the administration and operation of these gifts is dispersed throughout the body. In other words, no one individual operates all of the gifts, yet all of the gifts are present in the Body. The Holy Spirit bestows all spiritual gifts, and merely allows individuals to operate them. When we are yielded vessels and operate our diverse gifts, the entire body profits.

We observe that from the beginning, God established the principle of diversification. He decided before man sinned (before He ever suffered any loss), that He didn't want to have all His eggs in one basket. That was part of His reasoning for creating both man and woman. God did not lack confidence in His investment. He was merely ensuring the likelihood of a profitable return by distributing His investment in such a manner that the parts could work together. God has a portfolio approach as well. The Holy Spirit disperses spiritual gifts in the Body of Christ so that the well-being of the Church does not depend on any one individual. Make no bones about it — God is a God of diversification. He has uniquely selected and allocated His investments in a way that they can most beneficially work together. If we carefully select our investments and diversify our exposure by investing our time and resources in different things, then we are increasing the likelihood that we will generate a profitable return. I believe if it's good enough for God, it's good enough for me. What do you believe?

What Goes Around Comes Around

After we've paid our tithes, put our resources to work, and diversified our investments, it's time to sit back and wait for the profits to pour in, right? As faith would have it, it's not quite that easy. That's right — faith not fate. Every investment is built on faith. The Word of God tells us that faith is the substance of things hoped for and the evidence of things not seen (Heb. 11:1). That sounds like every investment I've ever made.

Take real estate for example. An individual invests in a piece of property with the expectation that when they decide to sell, the property will yield a greater price than what they paid for it. Take stocks or bonds. Anyone who invests in these securities has to have faith. As a stockholder you allow individuals that you've never met to manage a company that you own (even if it's just a small piece). In the case of bonds, you loan money to individuals you'll likely never meet. Chapter 7 examines these issues more closely, but I think we can all agree that investing requires faith. And guess what faith requires? Work! You may have been thinking that investing would do away with work once and for all. Forget it. Work is the system that God put in place for man to acquire resources and money. It also takes a lot of work to ensure that our investments turn out to be profitable. Let's see what type of work God requires to insure we end up with profitable investments.

> *2 Cor. 9:6-8* "But this I say, he which soweth sparingly shall also reap sparingly; and he which soweth boun-

tifully shall reap also bountifully. Every man according as he purposeth in his heart, so let him give; not grudgingly, or of necessity: for God loveth a cheerful giver. And God is able to make all grace abound toward you; that ye, always having all sufficiency in all things may abound to every good work:"

The principal of sowing and reaping is arguably the most universal principal in the natural world. If you don't remember any other principal in this book, I would encourage you to take heed to this one. Let's consider Einstein's theory of relativity. Einstein declared that for every physical action, there is an equal and opposite reaction. Scientific studies have proven that this principal is true. And well it should be, because it simply mirrors God's spiritual principal of sowing and reaping. Every word you speak, every decision you make, and every action you take causes a reaction in the natural world. If you read the passage from 2 Corinthians closely, you find an intriguing investment strategy. The scripture suggests that if you give bountifully, you will receive bountifully. Conversely, if you hold back by sowing sparingly, the Word declares that God will hold back things from you. In other words, successful investing is a function of your willingness to give.

You may be thinking that you can't afford to give what little you have to others. But read the passage again. God does not judge the amount you give *per se*. The Word is simply revealing to us that God rewards us according to what we purpose in our hearts. In other words, if we give out of a sincere desire to help others, God will reward us abundantly. God will never make you share what you have with others. However, if that's your resolve, I wouldn't expect much to come pouring your way out of the windows of heaven. The last part of the passage is powerful. It states that God is able to make all grace abound toward you. In chapter 1 we defined *grace* as all of

God's power and attributes working on our behalf. The Word tells us God has the ability, but it is our giving that unleashes the power of His grace in our lives.

Now, back to *work*. If you're honest with yourself, you know it is hard work to give with a cheerful heart — and that, quite frankly, is the catch. Notice that the Word clearly says that we should not give reluctantly or out of necessity, which means expecting something in return. It tells us that God rewards a cheerful giver. So the only way you can expect an abundant reward is if you give cheerfully. Some people have investments that are under water right now simply because they're selfish. They are unwilling to share God's blessings with others. In turn, God will not allow them to gain more. It's just that simple. Some people will tell you to give until it hurts. That is only partially true. You have to give until it doesn't hurt anymore. You have to give until it hurts not to give. When giving becomes second nature, you will witness investment returns like never before. God blesses you abundantly because He knows that He can trust you to help others.

Share the Wealth — God's Third Golden Rule

Luke 6:38 "Give and it shall be given unto you; good measure, pressed down, and shaken together, and running over, shall men give into your bosom. For with the same measure that ye mete withal, it shall be measured to you again."

The third and final golden rule is fully revealed in this verse: give and it shall be given unto you. Again, we're not just talking about money. God's entire economic system is based on giving. Think about it. He created the whole world and gave it to you. When man was lost, He came in the form of man and gave His life. God loves us so much that He can't help but give us things. However, as a responsible father He ensures that we are mature enough to handle the things He provides for us. We show our level of maturity in our ability to share and provide for others. God's system is so awesome that when you give, the returns are exponential. His Word declares that the return we receive will be overflowing. Other men will give to us richly because of God's favor upon our lives. Finally, you don't have to be rich to give. It just has to come from your heart. You can give your way out of poverty and into prosperity. God's grace truly is sufficient. I implore you to unleash the power of God's grace on your investment portfolio and experience what God's investment strategy has to offer.

Start Planting!

SEEDS FOR YOUR SOIL

Put God First: Matthew 6

1. What should be the first priority of every believer?

2. What is the result of putting God first?

3. Should believers worry about the future?

Pay God First: Malachi 3

1. What do we often withhold from God?

2. Why is it important that we invest in the Church?

3. How does God reward a faithful giver?

Diversity: 1 Corinthians 12

1. Do we all have the same abilities?

2. Do we all have the same responsibilities in the Church?

3. Why does God give us different talents and different responsibilities?

The Cheerful Investor: 2 Corinthians 9

1. What happens when we invest sparingly?

2. What happens when we invest bountifully?

3. What should our attitude toward giving be?

4. What is God's response when we have the right attitude toward giving?

The Power of Giving: Luke 6:27-38

1. What types of people should we give to?

2. What is the result of giving with a pure heart?

CHAPTER 6

Protecting God's Investment and Protecting Your Investment

Biblical Principles Regarding Wealth Preservation

If You Want to Be Wealthy, You've Got to Act Like It!

The Word of God tells us that as a man thinketh in his heart, so is he (Prov. 23:7). In short, that means you are what you think. Since we are all thinking wealthy at this point, it is only a matter of time before the riches start pouring in. The catch is, when you start thinking like the wealthy, you've got to start acting like the wealthy.

I read an interesting article recently that revealed something that may come as a surprise to many. It was an exposé on NFL football players. The article noted that the vast majority of NFL players are in financial ruin four to five years after retiring from the game. Many players sign multimillion dollar contracts. Admittedly, the career of the average NFL player is relatively short, around 5 years or so. However, with millions of dollars and a sound investment strategy, you'd think they'd be set for life. To be fair, I'm not picking on NFL players. My hunch is that this is largely true for most professional athletes and entertainers.

So where does the problem reside? I'll give you a hint. It begins with the way they think and it is manifested in their actions. Having money doesn't necessarily make you rich and it certainly doesn't make you wealthy. Individuals who quickly earn large sums of money often lack the capacity to think or act wealthy. They have the symbols of wealth, but they still behave as if they're poor. By *poor* I do not mean impoverished. These individuals exercise poor judgment and poor financial management, which results in the misuse of resources. The misuse of resources eventually leads to poverty, which is much like the case of the unprofitable servant who exercised poor financial management. His lord took away the money he had given him and gave it to the servant that invested wisely. This brings us to our final lesson regarding wealth creation. This is the lesson of wealth preservation.

Why Settle for Rich When You Can Be Wealthy?

Becoming rich is nice, but it isn't enough. If a person is rich, it generally means that person has an abundance of possessions. However, wealthy means more than just abundance. Do you know that you can have abundance and still not have enough? We can define *wealthy* with one simple word: ample. Wealthy individuals have resources that are generously sufficient to satisfy every need they have presently and in the future.

> *Eccl. 5:18-19* "Behold that which I have seen: it is good and comely for one to eat and to drink, and to enjoy the good of all his labour that he taketh under the sun all the days of his life, which God giveth him: for it is his portion. Every man also to whom God hath given riches and wealth and hath given him power to eat thereof, and to take his portion, and rejoice in his labour; this is the gift of God."

This verse helps us more fully understand the difference between becoming rich and becoming wealthy. The scripture suggests that it is both good and acceptable to enjoy the benefits we reap from our labor. So if God has blessed you such that your labor generates riches, don't let some narrow-minded believer tell you that you cannot enjoy the fruit of your labor. However, there are two caveats. First, the scripture states that the riches come from God. This is an important point because only riches that come from God will stand the test of time. Many individuals can't hold on to riches because they didn't get them according to God's plan. I'll let you in on a little secret. It is no use trying to preserve wealth that God never intended for you to have. This is why the Word of God declares that the wealth of the sinner is laid up for the just (Prov. 13:22). The sinner chooses his or her own path to riches as opposed to seeking God's plan. This is a one-way ticket to financial ruin. As believers, if we deviate from God's plan, we will suffer the same consequences.

Remember Deut. 8:18? "Thou shalt remember the Lord thy God: for it is He that giveth the power to get wealth..." This verse brings us to our second caveat. God gives us the power to get wealth. My point is that we can't stop once we acquire riches. The athletes and entertainers acquired riches for a short period of time. But riches alone will run out. That is why believers needn't settle for just being rich. Rich is just a pit stop on the way to wealthy. Many people confuse wealth with riches. They think they have enough, but they merely have a lot. Wealthy people have riches, but they don't define themselves as rich. The wealth they have actually produces riches. This is the way God works. He gives us a wealth of gifts, talents, and abilities. When used properly, this spiritual wealth produces riches both naturally and spiritually. However, if we fail to preserve the wealth God so freely gives us, we end up naturally and spiritually bankrupt.

Troublemakers

If you grew up in a church similar to my first church home, the preacher likely suggested that God has trouble with rich people. Now that was a tough pill for me to swallow because I wanted to acquire riches. I still do! But I swallowed the preacher's suggestion anyway. Then a revelation came! God actually does have trouble with many rich people. I didn't say He has trouble with riches. He merely has trouble with rich people. Let me show you what I'm referring to.

> *Matt. 19:23-25* "Then said Jesus unto His disciples, Verily I say unto you, that a rich man shall hardly enter into the kingdom of heaven. Again it is easier for a camel to go through the eye of a needle, than for a rich man to enter the kingdom of God. When the disciples heard it, they were exceedingly amazed, saying, Who then can be saved?"

Jesus told His disciples that it would be hard — not impossible — for a rich man to enter the kingdom of heaven. Let's define the *kingdom of heaven*. The Bible tells us that the kingdom of heaven is in the hearts of men. So this verse is not speaking of a physical place. My pastor defines the kingdom of heaven as the sovereign rule of God in the human heart. In other words, you enter the kingdom of heaven when you give your heart to God and He controls your life. Jesus also says, "Again it is easier for a camel to enter the eye of a needle than for a rich man to enter the kingdom of God."

"The eye of a needle" is not what most people think. This term was actually used to describe a type of entrance at a city gate. A camel would have to get down on all fours to pass through this small entrance. Since camels didn't like being in this position, it was a difficult process. The kingdom of God refers to God's domain. So Jesus was essentially saying that it would be very difficult for rich men to enter into God's presence.

God's trouble with rich people comes down to priorities. Far too often their desire for money and material things becomes their primary focus. Their love for money prevents them from allowing God to reign in their lives. If you don't have the right relationship with God it is easy to confuse material things with happiness and security. This false sense of comfort causes many who have riches to believe that they don't need God. The only thing worse than the lack of a personal relationship with God is the belief that you don't need one. True happiness and security can only come from God. God requires us to seek Him first. If we do this, then the riches generally follow. However, if we fail to put God first in our lives, we are definitely asking for trouble.

Valuable Advice

Let's face it. Jesus was tough on rich folks. But as He told His disciples on another occasion, to whom much is given, much is required (Luke 12:48). Jesus was tough on rich folks because He had high expectations of them. Unfortunately, many of the individuals God has richly blessed have fallen short of His expectations. However, if you have aspirations of building and preserving wealth, all is not lost. The disciples questioned how any rich person could receive salvation. Jesus responded by letting them know that with God all things are possible (Matt. 19:26). Christianity is not a poor man's religion; it is a lifestyle for those who are blessed and highly favored. The Word of God provides clear instruction for those with riches.

> 1 *Tim.* 6:17-19 "Charge them that are rich in this world, that they be not highminded, nor trust in uncertain riches, but the living God, who giveth us richly all things to enjoy; That they do good, that be rich in good works, ready to distribute, willing to communicate (share); Laying up in store for themselves a good foundation against the time to come, that they may lay hold on eternal life."

85

God didn't leave it up to us to figure out how to behave when we acquire riches. He knew most of us wouldn't know how to act. God gives specific guidance to those with riches because it is essential that they act responsibly. The first thing that God warns about is being conceited. God knows as soon as people get some money they tend to get an attitude. They start to develop an exaggerated opinion of themselves, believing they are better than others. Even more detrimental, they believe that they don't need God. The Word clearly tells us that it is God who gives us richly all things to enjoy. Furthermore, we are not to look down on others. It is quite the contrary. God gives us riches to enable us to do His will and share with others.

Rich Men, Not Wealthy Men Have Trouble Entering the Kingdom of Heaven

God makes clear distinctions between riches and wealth. We noted earlier that it is God who gives us the power to get *wealth* (Deut. 8:18), yet He tells us not to trust *uncertain riches* (1 Tim. 6:17). He tells us that a *rich* man shall hardly enter into heaven (Matt. 19:23), but God brings His chosen people to a *wealthy place* (Ps. 66:12). I'm not suggesting that wealthy people always get it right. However, I would suggest that God desires to use those that are disciplined enough to generate and preserve wealth. The Bible is filled with examples of wealthy believers, such as Abraham, Jacob, Job, Joseph, and David. What do all these men have in common?

> *Ps. 112:1-3* "Blessed in the man that feareth the Lord, that delighteth greatly in His commandments. His seed shall be mighty upon the earth: the generation of the upright shall be blessed. Wealth and riches shall be in His house: and His righteousness endureth forever."

The passage lets us know that every man that serves the Lord and keeps his commandments shall be blessed. Notice it says that wealth *and* riches will be in the Lord's house. As believers, we are entitled to an inheritance of the wealth and riches that are in the Lord's house. Abraham, Jacob, Job, Joseph, and David feared God and allowed Him to lead them. Their faith and obedience allowed God to make them wealthy beyond their wildest dreams. Obedience allows you to turn riches into wealth and your faith has the power to make you wealthy beyond your wildest dreams. More importantly, your faith gives you access to the kingdom of heaven and allows God to reign in your life.

The Art of War

Now that we can fully appreciate what it means to be wealthy, let's get on with the business of wealth preservation. Preservation is derived from the root word *preserve*, which simply means to protect or keep intact. In turn, wealth preservation implies a course of action that sustains wealth. God gives believers the power to get wealth. This is because we require a wealth of natural and spiritual resources to accomplish His plan for our lives. As investors, we are responsible for both producing and preserving wealth. Our God-given resources are precious, and we must protect them.

The Bible warns us that we are at war against principalities, powers, and rulers of darkness (Eph. 6:12). These forces are working overtime to prevent us from accomplishing God's plan for our lives. One of the tactics the enemy employs to prevent us from accomplishing God's will is cutting off our supply. Anyone who knows anything about war knows that this is a common tactic. Wealth is the sum total of our resources. God charges believers to preserve wealth so that we have resources in our time of need. God doesn't leave the outcome of His plan to our discretion. He goes as far as to instruct us to preserve wealth for the next generation of the Lord's army. His Word tells us that a good man preserves enough wealth for his grandchildren (Prov. 13:22). God always intended for wealth preservation to be an essential part of His plan for our lives.

Wealth Preservation for Dummies

I am fond of saying that there are two ways to do everything: there's God's way and then there is the wrong way. You'd think that after several thousand years man would give in and do things God's way. Unfortunately, that just isn't the case. Let's take a look at man's strategy for preserving wealth and see if we can unlearn a thing or two.

> *Luke 12:16-19* "The ground of a certain rich man brought forth plentifully: And he thought within himself saying, What shall I do because I have no room where to bestow my fruits? And he said, This will I do: I will pull down my barns, and build greater (I won't share what God has blessed me with); and there will I bestow all my fruits (material things) and goods (riches). And I will say to my soul (myself), Soul, thou hast much goods laid up for many years (I have enough); take thine ease (stop working), eat (consume), drink (lose focus) and be merry (party)."

This rich man was blessed abundantly and his investments produced plenty. His investments produced so much that he didn't have room to store his goods. So he devised what he thought was a good plan. He decided that he would tear down his current storage facilities and build even bigger ones. How many of us have thought that way at one time or another? How many people actually thought that this was a good plan when they first read it? The thought of sharing never occurred to the rich man. It seems easy to criticize, but how many times has God blessed us with abundance and we've failed to share with others?

This man's plan was to hoard everything he could in order to retire. He even says to himself that he has enough to live for many years. (He soon discovers that while he thought he had enough, he merely had a lot.) The first thing he planned to do was stop working. After which he planned to eat, drink, and party like there was no tomorrow. This sounds strangely similar to the so-called American dream. This system of wealth preservation is spreading all over the world. Our system of wealth preservation often sadly boils down to self-gratification. Let's see what God had to say about this plan.

> *Luke 12:20-21* "But God said unto him, Thou fool (a person who lacks judgment or discipline), this night thy soul shall be required of thee: Then whose shall those things be, which thou hast provided? So is he that layeth up treasure for himself (has a selfish plan), and is not rich toward God (does not follow God's plan)."

Talk about bursting your bubble. This man was prepared for a life of leisure and partying, but God puts an end to it all. God tells the rich man that on that very night he was going to die. I'm not sure what you think, but I'd say that any plan that ends in death is a bad plan. Where did he go wrong? The answer is simple. He misused the resources that God gave him. The scripture tells us that the ground of the rich man brought forth plentifully. In other words, it was God's doing, not his. God saw fit to bless this man so that he could do a work for God. The operative word being *work*. God didn't have retirement plans in his future. Consider this: many individuals who retire pass away shortly thereafter. Their lives lose the sense of purpose. Once the rich man decided that he would no longer make himself available to be used by God, God required his life. This gives new meaning to the phrase use it or lose it.

On the surface, it appeared that the rich man was, in fact, preserving his wealth. The problem was not so much his actions but his attitude. God wants us to protect the wealth that He gives us, but He does not want us to hoard it. Nothing about the rich man's actions suggest that he cared about anyone but himself. And nothing about his actions suggest that he considered the will of God. The final verse warns us about being selfish. God's plan for your life will always involve others. The primary purpose for wealth preservation is to accomplish God's will. Had the rich man considered this, he would have not only preserved his wealth, but he would have enjoyed the rich benefits of serving God. Our plan of wealth preservation must focus on God's will for our lives.

Your Greatest Supply of Wealth

Wealth is an abundance of riches, resources, or valuable possessions. With that in mind, I'd like to pose a question. What is our greatest supply of wealth? The answer is a little tricky, so I am going to help you out. God created everything, so He is the source of all wealth. However, in the natural world, your body is your greatest supply of wealth. Everything you need to survive in the natural world is contained in or processed by your body. Think about it. All of the wealth in the world actually comes from within us. God merely pulls it out of us. Bill Gates' multibillion dollar corporation began as a simple idea. Joseph's appointment to prime minister in Pharaoh's kingdom began with a dream. Likewise, your wealth or success comes from within.

> *1 Cor. 6:20* "For ye are bought with a price: therefore glorify God in your body and in your spirit which are God's."

Since man is God's greatest investment in the earth, then we are the embodiment of God's wealth — real live, walking, talking investments. That's why God is so concerned about the way we carry ourselves and the way we treat others. Notice that the scripture states that we "are bought with a price." The investment God made in us entitles Him to use our lives as He sees fit. But get this: He thinks so much of us that He won't use us without our permission. God gave all the wealth He created to man. Moreover, all of the wealth He plans to generate in the future He put inside man. God imparts knowledge to us through His Spirit. The Spirit requires a natural body to carry out God's will in the earth. His plan centers on pulling out the wealth that He put inside of man. This is precisely why He gives us His Spirit. God literally gets inside of us. How else is He going to get His return out of us?

> *1 Cor. 3:16-17* "Know ye not that ye are the temple of God, and that the Spirit of God dwelleth in you. If any man defile the temple of God, him shall God destroy; for the temple of God is holy, which temple ye are."

You may be wondering how this relates to wealth preservation, but the correlation should be clear. If we are going to talk about preserving wealth, then we must begin with our greatest supply of wealth. In the preceding passage, the Word of God stressed the importance of preserving our chief supply of wealth. The Word lets us know that our bodies are dwelling places of God. God actually values our bodies so much that He decided He would take up residence inside of us. Now that's awesome.

God gave us everything we need to develop and multiply His wonderful investment, but it's up to us to preserve it. The scripture warns us against defiling our bodies. Defile, as it is used in the preceding passage, is derived from the Greek word koinoo (koy-no'-o). It means to render unholy or unfit for use. This is in stark contrast to wealth preservation, which sustains or keeps in tact. God serves notice that He means serious business when it comes to His investment. The Word tells us that if we defile (fail to preserve) our temple (body), God will destroy us. I don't know about you, but that is reason enough for me to make wealth preservation a key part of my investment plan.

The Key to Wealth Preservation

> *Ps. 121:7* "The Lord shall preserve thee from all evil: He shall preserve thy soul."

Now after all of this build up, I bet you're expecting one whale of a strategy for wealth preservation. In fact, the strategy is simple: trust God. That's it. Case closed. Now the execution of the strategy is another thing altogether. Let's see what the Word of God has to say about preserving your greatest supply of wealth.

> *Rom. 12:1-2* "I beseech you therefore brethren by the mercies of a God, that ye present your bodies a living sacrifice, holy, acceptable unto God, which is your reasonable service. And be not conformed to this world: but be ye transformed by the renewing of your mind, that ye may prove what is that good, and acceptable, and perfect will of God."

To preserve your body, which is your greatest source of wealth, God gives you a simple instruction. He simply tells you to give your body to Him as a living sacrifice. God wants you to allow Him to direct your life. Because God made you and determined your purpose, He won't misuse you. God's direction will never cause you to defile yourself because His direction leads to holiness. If you allow God to direct your life, He will preserve your mind, which in turn allows you to preserve your body, which is your wealth. The Word goes on to warn us not to conform to the way unbelievers think, but to think as God thinks. Only then, can we truly carry out His will.

Preserving material wealth works the same as preserving the body. We must trust God and allow Him to lead us. The Bible tells us that if we acknowledge God in everything we do, then He will direct our paths (Prov. 3:6). This applies to our finances and investments also. The Word of God teaches us to practice good stewardship, seek godly advice, and invest wisely. These basic principles are all we require to effectively preserve our wealth. We began this chapter by highlighting examples of individuals who failed to preserve wealth. It is virtually certain that these individuals failed in at least one, if not all, of these areas. Nevertheless, their principal failure was simply a failure to trust God. God is the key to wealth preservation.

Start Planting!

SEEDS FOR YOUR SOIL

The Fruit of Your Labor: Ecclesiastes 5

1. Can money alone make us happy?

2. Does God want us to enjoy material things?

The Trouble with Riches: Matt. 19:16-26

1. Is it difficult for rich people to serve God?

2. Can a rich person serve God faithfully?

A Charge to the Rich: 1 Tim. 6:17-21

1. What charge does God give to rich people?

2. What happens when we share the things God richly blesses us with?

Wealth Preservation: Luke 12:16-32

1. What is the world's system for wealth preservation?

2. What's God's opinion of the world's system of wealth preservation?

3. When we invest with God is our future secure?

Preserve Yourself: Romans 12

1. What is the most important thing we can give to God?

2. How do we preserve ourselves?

PART III

TYPES OF INVESTMENTS

CHAPTER 7

ASSURANCE, NOT INSURANCE

Get Faith, It Pays

Investing Takes Faith

This is the third and final part of our journey, where the proverbial rubber meets the road. We will now examine various types of investments. With the Word of God as our guide, our objective is to effectively and productively put our God-given resources to work. Our goal is nothing short of abundant returns. Let's review some fundamentals. An investment is merely something received in exchange for a resource. Furthermore, an investment should provide a future benefit that exceeds the value of the resource that is given in exchange. Not everything that is presented as an investment qualifies as one. Moreover, some things that qualify as investments are actually poor investments at best. Our primary objective is to distinguish between various types of investments and allocate our resources appropriately.

Heb. 10:38 "Now the just (believers) shall live by faith:"

Every investment is based on faith. The dictionary defines faith as trust. To expound further, faith is complete trust in another. In the case of believers, we are referring to our complete trust in God. Trust depends on who and not what. We trust God because of who He is, not necessarily because of what He does. Interestingly enough, trust plays a major role in the investment process. Think about it. If you invest in a piece of real estate, you must take the seller's word with respect to the condition and worth of the property. Even if you do your own analysis, trust is still required for a transaction to be completed. Furthermore, if the property is held as an investment, you have faith that the value will increase over time. You must have faith in the future value of the property or you would never purchase it in the first place. Finally, if and when you decide to sell, you must have faith that the buyer has both the intention and means to pay the price that you are asking. The whole transaction, from beginning to end, is all about faith. Any type of investment you can think of requires a similar degree of faith.

> *Heb. 11:1* "Now faith is the substance (product) of things hoped for (our investment plan), the evidence (result) of things not seen (trust)."

The Word of God supports our notion regarding investments. The Word tells us that faith is the key to the things we hope for. In other words, the return on our investments comes as a result of our faith. Whenever we invest, we must trust others. More importantly, we must trust God. What does faith in God have to do with the return on our investments? I'm glad you asked.

> *1 Cor. 3:7* "So then neither is he that planteth any thing, neither he that watereth; but God that giveth the increase."

Remember this scripture. It tells us that the ones who do the planting and watering — the individuals who invest on our behalf — aren't really important. God causes our investments to bear fruit. Some people don't want to accept this truth because they don't want to invest in their relationship with God. Nonetheless, God controls all investment returns. Faith in God is the key to abundant investment returns. So while other things may appear to determine investment success, never choose form (appearance) over substance (faith).

Need a Little Insurance

Let's look at an asset that many individuals don't regard as an investment. Studies show that nearly 60 percent of American families own equities (directly or indirectly). Nearly 70 percent of American families own a home (real estate). While these numbers are relatively high, well over 90 percent of American families own some type of insurance. This makes insurance the most common investment among American households.

Many individuals don't view insurance as an investment, but let's go back to our definition and see if it qualifies. An investment is something received in exchange for a resource. Just about every type of insurance I can think of requires money. I have yet to be insured for free. On that basis, we can comfortably conclude that insurance passes part one of our test. We also stated that an investment should provide a future benefit that exceeds the value of the resource that is given in exchange. Now this one is a little tougher. There is no doubt that insurance (regardless of the type) provides future benefit. However, I am going to suggest that it is a rare case when the benefit received in the future outweighs the resource that is given up.

If we weigh the pros and cons, it seems fair to conclude that insurance qualifies as an investment. Unfortunately, in many cases it proves to be a poor investment. I believe that in general, people require less insurance, not more. I believe the average individual carries many types of insurance that they don't need. I believe that many individuals overpay for insurance. I also believe that there are certain critical events for which individuals often underinsure. Each of these problems is a result of our lack of knowledge concerning insurance and its proper use. Many of my beliefs concerning insurance are just that — my beliefs. I will be careful to distinguish my opinions from spiritual principles.

I don't have a bone to pick with insurance companies. These are for-profit enterprises, so their objective is to earn a profit for their shareholders, not their policyholders. If they built their business around enriching policyholders, they wouldn't be in the business for long. Studies by the National Insurance Consumer Organization show that over 90 percent of Americans carry the wrong types and amounts of coverage. I would submit that insurance often turns out to be poor investment because we lack knowledge concerning insurance. At least 90 percent of us anyway! Our lack of knowledge impairs our ability to allocate the appropriate amount of money to insurance. As a result, insurance generally provides the lowest return of any asset in our portfolio.

> *Prov. 18:15* "The heart of the prudent getteth knowledge; and the ear of the wise seeketh knowledge."

Solomon was the richest man of his time. That makes sense given he was the wisest man of his time. In the preceding scripture, Solomon writes that a prudent man seeks knowledge. This applies to every area of life and it most certainly applies to investments. So let's increase our knowledge of insurance. There are many types of insurance. Homeowner's insurance, medical insurance, and auto insurance are the most common types. However, there are other important forms of insurance, such as life insurance and disability insurance, that are also fairly common and very important. In addition, there are numerous minor policies, such as extended warranties or riders. You probably have a lot more insurance than you think. Complicating matters even further, there are countless variations of each type of insurance I've referred to.

> *Prov. 10:4* "He becometh poor that dealeth with a slack hand: But the hand of the diligent maketh rich."

Now, insurance companies are in the business of making money. Considering they profit from your policy, it doesn't take a genius to figure out that your objectives are somewhat different than theirs. When you buy insurance you are striking a deal. Each party wants to derive the maximum benefit. As with any deal, the more you know, the better off you are. That is why it is essential to be diligent when evaluating insurance policies. The average insurance company pays out 60 percent of the premiums they collect in the form of benefits. This fact should immediately tell you two things. One, most (not all) investments in insurance will have a negative return (on average you get back about sixty cents of every dollar you invest). Two, someone aside from Jane or John Doe is being enriched through this process.

Proverbs tells us that an individual who deals with a careless of lazy hand becomes poor. If you fail to take the time to learn about insurance, you are easy prey for a knowledgeable salesperson. Almost all insurance is sold through insurance agents that work on commission. This means the more insurance they sell, the more they get paid. In fact, they generally receive a percentage of the premium that the customer pays. Nearly half of the individuals who work for insurance companies are agents or brokers. That tells me a couple of things. There are a lot of people after my insurance dollar and many of these commission-generating agents may not have my best interest in mind.

I am not suggesting that insurance agents are bad people. However, it is in your best interest to learn as much as you can prior to sitting down to transact business. Insurance is not inherently bad. In fact, when used appropriately it is a beneficial complement to an investment portfolio. However, it is not an effective investment. Insurance is designed to spread or share risk, while investments are designed to profit from risk. If insurance is purchased to build wealth, it generally turns out to be an inferior investment. Ill-timed or uninformed purchases of insurance are arguably some of the worst investments. The remainder of this chapter establishes a framework for the appropriate use of insurance.

Think Big When It Comes to Insurance

Ps. 57:1 "Be merciful to me, O God, be merciful to me: for my soul trusteth thee: yea, in the shadow of thy wings will I make my refuge, until these calamities be overpast."

If you believe what I believe, then you know that faith in God is the best protection you can have. However, given that time and chance happen to us all (Eccl. 9:11), the right kind of insurance can't hurt. In his book *Personal Finance for Dummies*, Eric Tyson concludes that the primary purpose of insurance is to protect against big losses (calamities) that could result in financial ruin. This is in perfect agreement with much of the research I've done on the subject of insurance. It also clearly distinguishes the types of insurance an individual should purchase. Major medical, life, disability, business, liability, homeowner's and automobile insurance are the types of coverage that are most beneficial. It is especially important to be knowledgeable of your coverage when it comes to these critical areas. People often make the mistake of purchasing coverage that is insufficient or narrowly focused. The goal is to get most comprehensive policy given the amount you plan to spend.

The Life You Lead Is Not Your Own

John 15:13 "Greater love hath no man than this, that a man lay down his life for his friends."

Medical, homeowner's, and automobile insurance are likely to be a complement to your investment portfolio virtually all of your life. On the other hand, the need for life or disability insurance is largely dependent on your family status and financial position. It is unlikely that a single individual needs life insurance. It is also unlikely that a professional couple with no children needs life insurance. Wealthy individuals clearly don't need life insurance. So why do these types of individuals carry life insurance? The insurance companies do a great job at sales and marketing. Why else?

There are numerous circumstances in which the addition of life insurance to an overall portfolio is beneficial. For example, the sole provider for a single income household with multiple dependents may want to insure his or her life. In the event of the unthinkable, the family will have protection against financial ruin. I am not necessarily prescribing that individuals purchase life or disability insurance. I personally only carry minimum life and disability insurance provided by my employer. However, if you decide to purchase life or disability insurance, the greatest benefits accrue during your peak earning years (thirties and forties) and during the early years of raising a family. As you get older, life and disability insurance become much more expensive. I suggest building a healthy investment portfolio so that you won't need these types of insurance during your twilight years. Over time, your dependants become less dependent and, in return, require less protection. Life insurance isn't for your benefit anyway. It is designed to benefit the ones you love.

The Choice Is Yours

Deut. 30:19 "I call heaven and earth to record this day against you, that I have set before you life and death, blessing and cursing: therefore choose life, that both thou and thy seed may live."

If you decide that life insurance is right for you, I'd like to assist you in making one key choice. There are two generic forms of life insurance that are offered. Term insurance, which is plain vanilla life insurance, and cash value insurance, which combines death benefits and an investment feature. With term life insurance you pay an annual premium for a specified amount of coverage. For instance, Everlasting Life Co. may offer a thirty-year old in good health one million dollars of coverage for an annual premium of $500. As you get older your premiums increase because the likelihood that you will pass away also increases. This is why insurance has its greatest value in your early years. Cash value insurance also provides death benefits. However, the insurance company also takes some of your premium and invests it in a separate account for you. Therefore your policy has a cash value whether you die or not. This investment grows tax deferred much like a 401(k) plan or an IRA savings plan.

There's a lot more detail I could cover regarding the two types of plans, but I will leave further investigation to the prospective buyer. I firmly believe that term life insurance is the best choice, but for comparison sake allow me to offer a few points. For starters, the principal purpose (and in my opinion the only purpose) of insurance is to protect against unexpected events that might cause financial ruin. In this case, the event is death. Cash policies cost seven to eight times what term policies cost for an equal amount of coverage. So Everlasting Life Co. just bumped your $500 annual premium to $3,500. This includes your "good Samaritan" discount! I know what you're thinking. What about the investment that comes as part of that cash policy? I want to reiterate a point we made earlier. Insurance is designed to share risk. So your premiums are helping to offset the risk of thousands, potentially millions, of individuals that might pass away. By design, only a portion of your premium is being invested for your savings. The rest is contributed to a pooled account that covers many policyholders. I haven't even mentioned that the commission is generally more attractive on cash policies. So you are also sharing a little more of the wealth with your agent — probably more than you thought. If you do the research, the math speaks for itself. All I can say is: buyer beware.

You Could Pay More...but Why?

Luke 7:41-42 "There was a certain creditor (insurance provider) which had two debtors (policyholders): the one owed five hundred pence (had a 500 pence deductible), and the other fifty (50 pence deductible). And when they had nothing to pay (got into an accident), he frankly forgave (covered) them both. Tell me therefore, which of them will love him most (was better off)?"

Here's a piece of advice that a friend suggested to me some time ago. He told me that I should never choose a low deductible. In fact, he told me to take the highest deductible possible. I'd like to tell you that I followed his advice straight away, but I didn't. After several years of giving away my hard earned money, I finally saw the light.

My wife and I saved over 20 percent on the cost of our auto insurance by simply raising our deductible to the maximum amount. We saved nearly 10 percent on our homeowner's insurance by raising that deductible. To improve matters, God has allowed us to avoid accidents and kept our house standing on solid ground. I know some folks will suggest that this is a poor strategy if you are accident-prone. However, anyone who has been in a couple of fender benders will tell you that the insurance companies are careful to raise your rates when this occurs. The choice is yours, but math and experience suggest to me that the higher the deductible the better.

The Little Foxes

Song of Sol. 2:15 "Take us the foxes, the little foxes that spoil the vines:"

Here's my last bit of advice on insurance: insuring for small potential losses is a terrible investment. By small insurance policies, I am referring to things like warranties, repair plans, postal insurance, riders, credit card insurance, and so forth. These small policies appear attractive for one simple reason: they're small. Salespeople are adept at pointing out the large potential benefits you could receive for parting with a small amount of cash. What they are less forthcoming about is that these policies rarely pay off. Credit card insurance is seldom ever used, UPS delivers more often than not, and most products hold up well during the warranty period. These policies become little more than bad investments for you and almost pure profit for the company that sold them to you. Just think about it. If these policies were such great investments, why would every salesperson offer them to you?

I have never purchased service plans or extended warranties on products. I just assumed they were bad investments. However, as I learned more about insurance, I began to assess every insurance policy we had. I discovered a convenient car rental rider buried in my automobile insurance policy (Actually it was on the second page of the policy as plain as the nose on my face). My wife and I were shelling out $100 per year for separate riders that covered the two cars in our household. In the event of an accident, we were entitled to rent a car for no more that thirty bucks a day (I can tell you from experience this gets you a really small car). In five years time we have been involved in one accident and had to rent a car for about a week. You do the math! We received a $210 benefit and were on track to pay $500 over a five-year span. At the time we were involved in the accident, we only owned one car. If it happened today, it is likely that we could get by without renting a second car. I'm sure if you think hard, you can come up with countless small policies that have eaten away at your financial future. Remember, it's the little foxes that spoil the vine. Likewise it's the little expenses that will ruin your investment portfolio.

Raise Your Hands if You're Sure!

To conclude this discussion on insurance, I must share some essential spiritual principles regarding insurance. The root word of insurance is *sure*. The dictionary defines *sure* as certain or dependable. *Sure* is also defined as something or someone that is impossible to doubt. Insurance exists because there are many things in life that we are uncertain about, so we attempt to insure ourselves against the unknown. In essence, insurance is required because of lack of knowledge. There is an inverse relationship between knowledge and insurance. The less you know, the more insurance you need. Now here comes the revelation. God is the source of all knowledge. So the stronger your relationship with God, the less insurance you need. The Bible is knowledge. The Holy Spirit allows you to interpret the Word's knowledge. Furthermore, the Holy Spirit speaks to us and imparts knowledge if we maintain the proper relationship with God. God's Word is the only thing that we have that is sure. Let's see what Jesus said concerning God's Words.

> *Matt. 24:35* "Heaven and earth shall pass away, but my words shall not pass away (my words are sure)."

Now I don't want to confuse you. All the advice I gave you concerning insurance is both useful and relevant. So don't go out and cancel *all* of your policies. I want to drive home the point that you cannot rely on insurance. The word *insure* simply means to cover. In the event that something happens, we are reimbursed for our losses. The benefit we are entitled to is certain, but the circumstances of life are still full of uncertainty. Insurance doesn't prevent accidents; it merely reimburses us for the damages caused by them. Insurance can't prevent our home from burning down; it merely enables us to build another one in the event that it does.

What all of us really need is *assurance. Assurance* means confidence or boldness. Faith in God gives us assurance concerning the circumstances of life. Assurance is what gives insurance value. Faith is complete trust in God. How do we get faith? I'm glad you asked. Faith is purely a result of what you know.

> *Rom. 10:17* "So then faith cometh by hearing, and hearing by the Word of God."

Now that we have uncovered the key to faith, let's talk about the cost. An assurance policy, which only comes from God, is definitely going to cost you something. In fact, it's going to cost you your life. I never told you that serving God was free. As we stated before, faith comes as a result of what you know. Acquiring the knowledge of God is going to cost you. Let's read from God's assurance policy.

John 8:12 "Then spake Jesus again unto them, saying, I am the light (knowledge) of the world: he that followeth me (gives his life to me) shall not dwell in darkness (ignorance or uncertainty), but shall have the light (knowledge) of life."

There is nothing that compares to the peace and joy that comes from serving God. Faith in God will give you all the assurance you need to achieve the great things God has planned for your life. Faith in God also gives you the assurance you need to become the investor that God intends you to be. The Bible declares that David was a man after God's own heart. A few verses from the Psalms of David tell us about the assurance of God.

Ps. 23:4-6 "Yea, though I walk through the valley of the shadow of death, I will fear no evil: for thou art with me (God is with me); thy rod and thy staff they comfort me. Thou preparest a table before me in the presence of mine enemies: thou anointest my head with oil (God blesses me); my cup runneth over (I have an abundance). Surely goodness and mercy shall follow me all the days of my life: and I will dwell in the house of the Lord for ever."

If you exercise faith in God, His grace and mercy will follow you all the days of your life. This assurance is all the insurance you'll ever need.

Start Planting!

SEEDS FOR YOUR SOIL

The Definition of Faith: Hebrews 11

1. How de we define faith?

2. What does faith enable us to understand?

3. What does faith give us the power to do?

Debt Forgiveness: Luke 7:40-43

1. Can we afford to repay the debt of sin that we owe?

2. What does Jesus do with the debt we owe?

Goodness and Mercy: Psalm 23

1. What role does God play in our lives?

2. What provisions does God make for us?

3. What happens when we find ourselves in trouble?

CHAPTER 8

Risk-Free Investments

How to Invest in a Sure Thing!

Is It Worth the Risk?

In the wonderful world of investments, it is assumed that all investors are risk-averse. In short, risk aversion implies that people don't like taking risks. In a more academic sense, the term risk aversion suggests that individuals prefer investments with low risk profiles. Recall the two types of risk: unique risk, which is mitigated by diversification, and market risk, which is outside of our control. In chapter 5, we concluded that the return on any investment is largely a function of taking on market risk. Interestingly enough, our carnal nature encourages us to avoid risk altogether.

> *Prov. 3:5-6* "Trust in the Lord with all thine heart; and lean not unto thine own understanding. In all thy ways acknowledge Him and He shall direct thy paths."

> *2 Cor. 5:7* "For we walk (live and invest) by faith and not by sight."

Why are we inherently risk-averse? I would submit that the answer is twofold. Risk aversion occurs naturally because it is part of our makeup. God deliberately designed us to be dependent on Him, one another, and our environment — in that order.

It is necessary to understand that risk aversion often limits our investment success. The Word of God declares that believers live according to faith. This word *faith* is the Greek word *pistis* (pis'-tis). This word is used throughout the New Testament and it means faith in God, Christ, or spiritual things. The Word implies that every decision we make should be based on trust in God. This includes investment decisions. The Word of God also tells us that we should not live based on how things appear. This is because looks can be deceptive. Many decisions in life require guidance by the Holy Spirit. The Holy Spirit picks up where our natural senses leave off. When we acknowledge God, He reveals the right course of action.

Investing mirrors our walk as believers. God has the power to do the impossible in our lives. However, it is our faith that unleashes the power of God. An investor needs faith to generate an abundant return. Lack of faith often prevents God from operating in our lives. Likewise a lack of faith often prevents us from pursuing profitable investments. The lack of faith is the second and more common aspect of risk aversion. This fear of the unknown, which is a failure to trust God, is the primary obstacle to our success as investors.

You've Got Nothing to Fear!

> *Matt. 4:4* "But He (Jesus) answered and said, It is written, Man shall not live by bread alone, but by every word that proceedeth out of the mouth of God."

God put all of His power in His Word. We know this in principle because the Word of God created all living things. In turn, God's Word is the essence of life. When you profess the Word of God, you give God's Spirit authority to operate in your life. The presence of God's Spirit is what gives you life. Death is merely the absence of God's Spirit. Moreover, when you live according to the Word of God, you are exercising faith. As we stated before, faith unleashes the power of God. Faith is a function of what and, more importantly, whom you know. When you have God's indwelling Spirit and understand the Word of God, then investing, which is stepping out on faith, comes naturally.

> *2 Cor. 4:13* "We having the same Spirit of faith, according as it is written, I believed, and therefore have I spoken; we also believe, and therefore speak;"

Why all this talk about the Holy Spirit? What does this have to do with investing? It's quite simple. One of the biggest obstacles to investing is risk aversion. We don't like uncertain outcomes. This fear of the unknown results in missed opportunities and subpar investment returns. Fear is the opposite of faith. Fear will cause you to abandon a business plan before it ever gets off the ground, and fear will cause you to avoid potentially lucrative investments.

> *2 Tim. 1:7* "For God hath not given us the spirit of fear; but of power, and love and of a sound mind."

The Holy Spirit gives us power, love, and a sound mind. A sound-minded individual operates on faith in the Word of God. This is why Jesus was the quintessential investor. He possessed God's Spirit, which is the Spirit of faith. Notice that the scripture tells us that God has not given us the spirit of fear. Fear is not a part of God's make-up. Like Jesus, every believer has the Spirit of faith. However, we must exercise our faith to become successful investors.

Enough Is Enough!

Rom. 12:3 "For I say, through the grace given unto me, to every man that is among you, not to think of himself more highly than he ought to think; but to think soberly, according as God hath dealt to every man the measure of faith."

The scripture states explicitly that God gives faith to "every man" — not every believer, not every good man. More specifically, it states that every man is given "the" measure of faith. It doesn't state that every man is given *some* faith. It doesn't state the every man is given *a* measure of faith. God didn't leave anyone out and He didn't discriminate. He provided each individual with the appropriate amount of faith.

We defined *faith* (*pistis*) as trust in God. I know some believers may struggle with my assertion that every man has "the measure of faith." We are all spirits wrapped in flesh. As spirits we are designed to operate like God. If you want to know how God operates just examine the life of Jesus. He operated in 100 percent faith. His spoken words caused change in the natural. The problem with unbelievers is not that they don't have faith, it's that they choose not to exercise their faith. After all, unbelief is simply the inability to exercise faith. The question is not whether or not an individual has faith. The question is whether they're going to use it.

What is "the" measure of faith? When God gives faith, He doesn't give an equal amount — He gives the right amount. The right or appropriate amount of faith differs from person to person. So there is no standard measure when it comes to faith. God gives you faith in proportion to the purpose He has determined for your life. Abraham was called to be the father of many nations. As such, he required a lot of faith. Peter was called to become the leader of the New Testament

Church, so he too required a lot of faith. God has given each one of us the requisite amount of faith to accomplish our mission in the earth. As such, "the" measure of faith is all the faith we need to fulfill God's plan for our lives.

We often equate equal with fair. However, the two don't necessarily have anything to do with one another. If I sent one individual to the store to purchase a gallon of milk and another person to purchase four gallons of milk, I wouldn't give them the same amount of money. The individual who has to purchase four gallons has a greater responsibility and thus a greater need. I would have to give this individual more money than the first for the individual to accomplish his or her task. It would hardly be fair to give each individual the same amount of money. The fair thing to do is to give the second individual four times the amount of money the first receives. God deals with faith the same way. God first determines His will for our lives. He then gives us enough faith to carry out His plan. We must simply obey the Word of God and accept that when it comes to "the" measure of faith, enough truly is enough.

Uncle Sam Wants You to Take a Little Risk

We'll begin with the low end of the risk spectrum. The remainder of this chapter focuses on risk-free investments, beginning with the characteristics of risk-free investments. This should provide a basic understanding of the nature and timing of investment returns. Next, we will identify various types of risk free investments. Finally, we will discuss some helpful strategies for utilizing this class of investments. My primary objective is to give an overview of this class of securities and provide a framework for evaluating treasuries as a potential investment alternative.

The U.S. government is the most reliable borrower in the world. This is based on the fact that the U.S. has never defaulted on its debt obligations. Given this history of consistent payments, debt instruments issued by the U.S. treasury are often referred to as risk-free securities. In reality, all securities have some degree of risk, but we will revisit that point a bit later. The U.S. Treasury offers three types of debt securities: bills, notes, and bonds. The primary difference among these debt securities is their term to maturity. Debt issued by the U.S. Treasury can have initial maturities that range from thirteen weeks to thirty years. Treasuries, the most common name for this class of securities, serve as the benchmarks against which all other debt securities are compared.

Treasuries are debt instruments. Simply put, investors agree to loan the government money. In the case of notes and bonds, investors receive a stated rate of interest. The borrower (government) agrees to pay the lender (investor) interest in return for his or her loan. At the end of an agreed upon time period, the government returns the investor the original amount borrowed. In the case of bills or zero coupon bonds, there are no interim interest payments. The investor pays a discounted price at the onset of the transaction and receives both interest and principal payments at maturity.

Key Bond Terms	
Par value	the amount an investor will receive at maturity
Interest rate	the return the borrower is paid for the loan
Maturity date	the date the loan agreement expires

There are a few basic terms that an investor must understand when investing in treasury securities. The *par value* is the face value of the security, which is the amount the issuer will repay the bondholder on the maturity date. Once a bond is issued, it trades at the appropriate market price. After issuance, the par value is only used to determine the interest payment, which brings us to our next term. The *interest rate* (or *the rate*) represents the return associated with the investment.

The rate is the return that the borrower agrees to pay in return for the loan. The rate is stated as a percentage and it is generally determined by market conditions. The rate is set at the time the bond is issued. Finally, all treasuries — and nearly all debt securities for that matter — have a fixed *maturity date*. This is the date when the loan agreement expires and the loan must be paid back in full.

Time to maturity is the primary feature that distinguishes the various types of treasuries. Treasury bills also differ from other treasuries given they do not provide interim interest payments; this is due to their short maturities. Instead, treasury bills are offered at a discount to their par value. For example, an investor may pay $9,800 for a 26-week treasury bill and receive the $10,000 par value for the security at maturity. The difference between the amount paid and the par value received at maturity is the interest that the investor receives for the 26-week loan. The table below presents the different securities issued by the U.S. government.

Types of Treasuries Issued by the U.S. Government			
	Par Value	Maturity Period	Interest Bills
Bills	$10,000	13-52 weeks	discounted
Notes	$1,000	1-10	semiannual
Bonds	$1,000	10 years	semiannual

There is no such thing as a truly risk-free investment. Even treasuries, which are backed by the U.S. government, are subject to market risk. When interest rates change, the value of treasury securities change. Specifically, when interest rates rise, the value of treasury securities fall. This is known as interest-rate risk. There is a second form of risk associated with treasury notes and bonds known as reinvestment risk. This means that when rates are falling, interest paid on treasury securities must be reinvested at these lower rates.

Treasury Strategy

It's time to talk strategy. Virtually every portfolio should have some percentage of stable investments. That is why treasuries are a meaningful asset class. However, the proportion of your portfolio devoted to treasuries or other low-risk investments depends on a few key factors, the first of which is time. The mix of assets in your personal portfolio is greatly affected by the time period over which you plan to invest.

As a general rule of thumb, the longer the period for investment, the more risk you can afford. For example, if you are thirty years old and you are saving for retirement, you may choose to own a large proportion of stocks and very little in the way of treasuries or other bonds. This is because over long periods of time, equities provide a greater return than bonds. Conversely, if you are fifty-five years of age and considering early retirement, you may want to choose to put a good deal of your nest egg in treasuries or other relatively stable investments. Remember, time, and not your age, is the primary consideration when it comes to investing. Parents often invest for their children's education. In the early years equities may be a more attractive choice. However, as time draws near for the child to begin college, these savings are likely best maintained in stable investments such as treasuries.

Suitability is another investment-strategy consideration. In short, an individual must determine if a particular type of investment is appropriate given their level of risk tolerance. For example, if you can't bear the thought of losing money in the short-run, equities probably aren't right for you. If you prefer liquid investments, real estate is not the best choice. If you are looking for eye-popping investment returns, then treasuries won't float your boat. Alternatively, if you prefer a modest return with very little risk, treasuries could be just the investment for you.

Financial position is another important consideration. Your financial position at any given time will dictate many of your investment options. Ever heard the phrase "it takes money to make money"? Individual treasury securities are sold in denominations of at least $1,000. Some are sold in denominations of $10,000. Fortunately for you and me, financial innovation has brought treasury investing to the land of the affordable. Treasury bond funds are a common and often preferable way to invest in treasury securities. They provide returns that are similar to actual treasuries and have added benefits. Treasury funds have lower investment minimums, often as low as $250. Unlike individual bonds, funds have no maturity date. Your interest payments can be automatically reinvested and the investment lasts for the life of the fund. In this way you are not limited to the bond maturity date. Finally, liquidating a fund position is generally easier than selling an actual treasury security. The growth of treasury mutual funds has made investing in treasury securities easy and affordable.

You Get What You Pay for

There are other types of low-risk investments. These include, but are not limited to, savings accounts, money market funds, savings bonds, and certificates of deposit. There are times when any or several of these investments may be a meaningful part of your investment portfolio. These investments provide stability of principal and some degree of return, but it is important to remember one principle. When it comes to investing, you get what you pay for. So if you pay for a limited amount of risk, you should expect a limited amount of return. I am not suggesting that these are bad investments. Quite the contrary. I own several of these types of investments myself. I simply want to put this investment class in the proper perspective. Low risk does not necessarily mean a sound investment. The quality of the investment is determined by the likelihood of meeting future need.

A Little Faith Goes a Long Way

> *Matt. 17:20* "And Jesus said unto them (His disciples), 'Because of your unbelief: for verily I say unto you. If ye have faith as a grain of mustard seed, ye shall say to this mountain, remove hence from yonder place; and it shall remove; and nothing shall be impossible unto you.'"

If you study the New Testament, you realize that Jesus stuck around long enough to develop some true investors. Jesus began His ministry with many followers, but over time the number dwindled. He eventually chose twelve disciples to accomplish His mission. He wanted to impart Kingdom principles that would be taught to believers. He wanted to establish His Church in the earth. Finally, He desired to restore man as the investors we were called to be. Now I want to take you back a bit to make my final point. In chapter 3 we recounted an occasion in Matthew 14 where Jesus feeds a multitude of people with just five loaves of bread and two fishes. Jesus demonstrated one of the principal qualities of an investor as He exhibited the ability to multiply resources. Like many of us, the disciples had trouble embracing a walk of faith. In spite of the life Jesus led before them, when it came to investing, the disciples still lacked faith. Let's see what Jesus said to His disciples.

> *Matt. 16:5, 8-9* "And when His disciples were come to the other side, they had forgotten to take bread... When Jesus perceived He said unto them, 'O ye of little faith, why reason ye among yourselves, because ye have brought no bread? Do ye not understand, neither remember the five loaves of five thousand and how many baskets ye took up?'"

Jesus questioned His disciples' ability to exercise faith. Jesus wasn't saying that they possessed a small amount of faith. He knew that God had given them all the faith they needed. He was merely saying that they exercised very little faith. God does not suggest we should live by faith, rather He requires that we live by faith. Just as we are looking for a return out of our investments, God is looking for a return out of our lives. The key to abundant returns in both cases is the application of faith. God wants the best for all of His children, but it is up to us to get the best out of ourselves. God put the best in you. Seek God through His Word. In investing or any aspect of your life, exercise faith and allow God to grant the increase.

Start Planting!

SEEDS FOR YOUR SOIL

Confidence in God: 2 Corinthians 5

1. Why can believers always be confident?

2. How do believers live their lives?

3. What happens to individuals when they accept Christ as their savior?

4. Why did Christ die for our sins?

The Measure of Faith: Romans 12

1. What gift should we present to God?

2. Why must we change our way of thinking?

3. What did God give to every man?

4. How does faith relate to our spiritual gifts?

You Can Move Mountains: Matthew 16-17

1. What power does Jesus give to His disciples?

2. How much faith do we need to exercise?

3. Can God do the impossible in our lives?

CHAPTER 9

RISKY INVESTMENTS

Greater Risk, Greater Reward!

Fear and Greed!

Warren Buffet is regarded as one of the greatest investors of the modern era. He has been quoted on occasion as describing the marketplace for investments as a tug of war between two forces. The two forces are appropriately described as the human emotions of fear and greed. He defines investment success in part as the ability to manage these divergent emotions. Fear is the principal enemy of investment success. It causes one to fail at the investment game before ever starting. Greed is public enemy number two in the world of investing. Greed can cause one to make unwise investment decisions that eventually result in investment ruin. Mr. Buffett believes that astute investors must be greedy when others are fearful and fearful when others are greedy. In simple terms, Mr. Buffett is suggesting that you will have a hard time finding investment success by following the crowd or being overtaken by emotion.

Matt. 7:13-14 "Enter ye in at the strait gate: for wide

is the gate, and broad is the way, that leadeth to destruction, and many there be which go in thereat: Because strait is the gate, and narrow is the way, which leadeth unto life, and few there be that find it."

Fear and greed are often at the root of bad choices. Many individuals live their lives in fear of what other people think. They are defined by the opinions and expectations of others. They live their lives to please others rather than to please God. Others lead their lives controlled by their appetite. They are overcome with greed and live to satisfy their flesh. They live to please themselves as opposed to living a life that is pleasing to God. In either case, life becomes fruitless and unfulfilling. Worse yet, the end of the individual that doesn't live to please God is destruction.

There is an overwhelming temptation to follow the crowd when it comes to investing. The slightest sign of market turbulence unsettles most investors. Moreover, individuals are far too easily persuaded by popular get-rich-quick schemes or seemingly fail-proof investments. These are just small examples of the broad way of investing that will lead to portfolio destruction. This is why it is important that believers follow the principles laid out in the Word of God as they pertain to investing. This is even more critical when it comes to risky investments. Remember, the greater reward is preceded by the assumption of greater risk.

Risky Business

Risk, simply defined, is the possibility of loss or injury. For example, every time I go for a drive in my car there is a risk that I could be involved in an accident. More specifically, there is a risk that my property (the automobile and its contents) could be damaged. More importantly, there is the risk that I could suffer bodily harm. Investing is not much different. Every time I invest in an asset or a security, there is a chance that I will lose some of my initial investment. Moreover, there is a chance that I could lose all of my investment. I chose to focus on the definition of risk in this chapter because when dealing with certain risky investments, it is vitally important to understand the implied risk.

Individuals often don't have a clear understanding of the risks involved with a given investment. Many of you are homeowners and a home is a fairly common investment. When purchasing a home, we tend to spend most of our time focused on the monthly payment. For many, the purchase decision simply comes down to the ability to make the mortgage payment. I want to let you in on a little secret. Just because you currently have enough money to make the payment, doesn't mean you can afford the home. The cost of owning a home significantly exceeds the cost of renting. People are quick to point out the benefits of writing off the interest portion of your mortgage payment for tax purposes. However, people are much more reticent when it comes to the incremental expenditures that go along with owning a home. The difference becomes glaringly apparent the first time the roof leaks or a water pipe bursts.

The facts are simple. Home ownership costs much more than you think. Furthermore, individuals categorically underestimate expenditures associated with the furnishing and maintenance of a home. Remember, it's always important to consider the cost of investing to determine whether the potential benefit of an investment outweighs the expected cost. If an individual assumes a mortgage that they are later unable to afford, the consequences are quite dire. Not only will they lose their home and all they've invested in it, but their family will also have to endure some trying circumstances. Most individuals don't look at buying a home as a risky investment. However, it is just that. Our risk assessment must be careful and thorough. Investing is truly rewarding and it is specifically what we were created to do. Nevertheless, investing is risky business and must be treated as such.

Jesus Is My Everything

Before we jump into specific types of risky investments, I want to do away with a couple of faith myths. Faith has been our primary focus because it is the key to investing success. Nevertheless, we have to truly understand faith and how it works to experience its benefits in our lives. Faith in God is demonstrated by obeying Him. Faith can never be based on what He does, but must be based on who He is. When we put the Word of God first in every aspect of our lives, we are truly living by faith.

> *Matt. 9:27-30* "And when Jesus departed thence, two blind men followed Him, crying and saying, 'Thou son of David, have mercy on us.' And when He was come into the house, the blind men came to Him: and Jesus said unto them, 'Believe ye that I am able to do this?' They said unto Him, 'yea, Lord.' Then touched He their eyes, saying, 'according to your faith be it unto you.' And their eyes were opened."

This account of the two blind men exemplifies the true exercise of faith. The two blind men cried after Jesus identifying Him as the son of David. They recognized Him as the Messiah who had been prophesied of from the days of old. Their request was based on who they believed Him to be. When Jesus stopped to address the blind men, He asked them a simple question: Do you believe that I am able to do this? Notice that the focus was on His ability to perform the request as opposed to whether or not it could be done. They answered yes and once again referred to Him as Lord. Jesus said to them, "according to your faith be it unto you." This statement implies that because the blind men had faith in Him, they received what they were asking for. Moreover, it suggests that His authority to work on our behalf depends on the amount of faith we exercise. Jesus requires your faith in order to operate in your life.

You Need More Than Faith to Get the Job Done

Many preachers today have embraced a message of prosperity. Name it, claim it, believe it, and you can have it! Sounds pretty compelling. While God certainly wants His people to prosper, He is most concerned about our relationship with Him. Moreover, successful investing is more than just naming and claiming things. I have heard many born-again believers talk about faith, but I've seen few walk in it. This suggests to me that faith alone may not lead to investing success. Let's see what the Word has to say about it.

> *James 2:20* "But wilt thou know, O vain man, that faith without works (actions) is dead (inactive)?"

How can an individual have dead faith? The refusal to work for God and obey His Word is only part of it. The truth is that faith was never intended to operate alone. There are some other things that must go along with faith in order for it to be effective.

> *2 Pet. 1:5-9* "And beside this, giving all diligence, add to your faith virtue; and to virtue knowledge; And to knowledge temperance; and to temperance patience; and to patience godliness; And to godliness brotherly kindness; and to brotherly kindness charity. For if these things be in you, and abound, they make you that ye shall neither be barren nor unfruitful in the knowledge of our Lord Jesus Christ. But he that lacketh these things is blind, and cannot see afar off, and hath forgotten that he was purged from his old sins."

This passage is essential for understanding the practical application of faith. This book is believed to be the last book written in the New Testament. One of its major aims is to denounce false teaching. It would be false indeed to teach that believers need only proclaim faith to be effective investors. The true exercise of faith is dependent on our ability to exhibit the character traits of our Lord Jesus Christ. Jesus lived by faith. Moreover, He exhibited the qualities that this passage of scripture refers to. Jesus was the embodiment of virtue, knowledge, temperance, patience, godliness, brotherly kindness, and charity. These qualities enabled His faith to operate effectively. It was His willingness to embrace these character traits and add them to His faith that made Him the quintessential investor. Likewise, our willingness to add these qualities to our faith will determine our investing success.

Take a Little More Risk

With a clear understanding of both risk and faith, it's time to discuss some of those risky investments. Our discussion includes bonds, equity investments, and indirect and direct investments in real estate.

Bond Ownership

When investors think of bonds, they generally think of stability and safety. However, the universe of bonds range from low-risk treasuries to high-risk junk bonds. Therefore bond investors must understand the risks associated with various types of bonds. Since chapter 8 covered many of the basic characteristics of bonds, I will forgo that here. Again my objective is to highlight the relevant classes of bonds and discuss their investment merit.

Bond investors are lenders who provide capital to borrowers. In the case of treasuries, the borrower is the U.S. government. Likewise other large institutions regularly borrow from investors; that is, they issue debt. There are three significant classes of borrowers. The U.S. government, municipalities (states, cities, counties, townships), and corporations account for the majority of debt issuance. This chapter focuses on municipal bonds and corporate bonds since we covered treasury securities in the previous chapter.

Municipal Bonds

Municipalities regularly borrow money to supplement their operating budgets. This helps them cover things like public services and government overhead. Municipalities also borrow money for special projects, such as highways, stadiums, and bridges. Although it would be nice if people felt it were their civic duty to loan their local governments money, this simply isn't the case. However, municipal bonds are free from federal taxes and often times free from state and local taxes. This tax-deferred component is what gets investor's attention. Municipal bonds are particularly attractive to individuals in high tax brackets.

There are two categories of municipal bonds: general obligation bonds, which are used to supplement the operating budgets of local governments; and revenue bonds, which are used to fund special projects, such as highways and bridges. General obligation bonds are secured by the taxing power of the local government. In other words, if the government is in danger of missing a payment, they have the option to raise taxes. Conversely, the revenue associated with a particular project secures revenue bonds. For example, a revenue bond for a new toll road is repaid with the toll revenue generated by those who use the toll road. As you might imagine, revenue bonds are a bit riskier and, on average, provide higher yields. Municipal bonds, regardless of type, have relatively low default rates.

Corporate Bonds

Corporations borrow money to pay for operating expenses, fund expansion, or finance acquisitions. Corporations must rely on their ability to generate profits to repay lenders. Inasmuch as some corporations are highly profitable and others go bankrupt, the risk among corporate bonds varies greatly. While this makes investing in corporate bonds complicated, the risk is offset by higher returns. As you might expect, corporations pay higher interest rates than treasuries and municipal bonds. Furthermore, corporations with greater business risk must pay higher yields on their debt than corporations with less business risk.

Which One to Choose?

One of the biggest challenges for a bond investor is choosing between the numerous classes and maturities of bonds. A single corporation may have as many as ten or twenty outstanding maturities of bonds. If you multiply this across the breadth of issuers, you can get a sense of the difficulty. Further complicating matters, there is an array of risks associated with the bonds of different issuers. The same issuer may even have different types of bonds that carry vastly different risks. It is nearly impossible for the average individual to identify and access these risks. So how does one choose? Very carefully. However, you'll be delighted to know that there are services to aid investors in the selection process.

Rating services are in the business of measuring the risks associated with various types of bonds. The most popular services are Standard and Poor's (S&P) and Moody's. These companies examine the financial condition of bond issuers. They consider factors like the industry that the company operates in as well as the company's profitability and growth prospects. The services also compare the companies to other issuers in similar businesses. Rating agencies rate international bonds, municipal bonds, and corporate bonds. U.S. treasuries are not rated because they are presumed to be free from default risk. Rating services issue credit ratings that give investors a proxy for the risk associated with a particular bond issue. The ratings range from AAA, the highest quality rating, to C, the lowest quality rating. The rating services regularly update bond ratings as the financial condition of a respective issuer changes.

Bond Ratings		
Moody's	S&P	Rating
Aaa	AAA	Best quality
Aa	AA	High quality
A	A	High – medium quality
Baa	BBB	Medium quality
Ba	BB	Some speculative element
B	B	Low Quality
Caa	CCC	Poor Quality
Ca	CC	Highly speculative quality
C	C	Lowest-rated
D		In default

Bond Strategy

The first important consideration is time horizon. Bonds are particularly attractive for mature investors or wealthy investors who are looking for respectable returns and stability of principal. However, municipal bonds and corporate bonds offer risky issues that may appeal to investors looking for returns superior to treasuries. Bonds are also attractive during periods of market volatility. Generally speaking, most classes of bonds outperform stocks during turbulent markets. Bonds are also relatively attractive once you have achieved an investment objective or are close to liquidating an investment portfolio. For example, if you are saving for a child's ed-

ucation you may decide to switch to bonds as the time for enroll-
ment approaches.

Suitability is the second consideration. Investors should be particularly cautious about low quality bonds. Bonds with investment
ratings of Ba/BB or lower are considered below investment grade
and are inappropriate investments for investors who are risk
averse. Investors must also make sure that the types of bonds they
have chosen complement their investment needs. For example, an
individual looking for good returns who has a reasonable tolerance for risk is better off investing in high quality corporate bonds
as opposed to treasuries.

Financial position is the other consideration. Wealthy investors
are better off investing in municipal bonds because of their tax advantage. An individual in a 36 percent tax bracket will get a better
return buying a municipal bond yielding 7 percent than he or she
would buying a corporate bond yielding 10 percent. This is because
after paying taxes on the corporate bond, the effective yield would
be 6.4 percent [$10\% \times (1 - 0.36)$]. Conversely, a middle class individual in a 28 percent marginal tax bracket would be better served
by the corporate bond because he or she would have an after-tax
yield of 7.2 percent [$10\% \times (1 \quad 0.28)$]. Bond investing requires a
substantial amount of disposable income. Like treasuries, most
bonds are sold in denominations of $1,000 or more. It is difficult
for the average individual to maintain a diversified bond portfolio.
However, the growth of bond funds has made investing in bonds
easy and affordable.

Equity Ownership

I have spent the past four years working in equity sales. Moreover, I
have spent much of the last ten years studying the financial markets,
analyzing stocks, and investing personally and professionally. Our
study of equities includes common stocks, but the area of equity in-

vesting is much broader. *Equity* can be viewed as residual ownership. Whether referring to a business or a piece of property, the equity ownership is the value remaining after all debts are paid. Equity investors take on substantial risk because they can only receive a return after creditors are paid off. For example, you don't truly own your home until your mortgage is paid off. You merely have equity in your home. The bank owns a portion and you own the rest. This concept applies to all equity investments.

Common Stock — The People's Choice

The most familiar and widely held form of equity investment is common stock. Many individuals own common stock either directly in an investment account or indirectly through mutual funds or pensions. In chapter 3 we noted that common stock represents partial ownership in a corporation. In exchange for your hard-earned money, you receive a residual claim on the profits of the corporation you invest in. That means investors are entitled to a share of the remaining profits once the company's creditors are paid off. It is important to note that ownership does not mean control. In fact, most investors that own common stock have little or no control over the company they invest in. Control rests with those who either founded the company or have been chosen to manage the company. In most cases, common stock holders are in most cases given the right to vote on important issues. However, the management controls the day-to-day operation of the company.

Investments in common stocks provide several attractive characteristics for investors. Common stocks are traded on public market exchanges and, as a result, are easy to buy and sell. They involve more risk, but over long periods of time investments in common stocks consistently outperform bonds. While superior performance is in no way guaranteed, a well-diversified stock portfolio generally yields handsome returns over an investor's lifespan. Stocks can have an infinite lifespan. As long as the company stays in business, the life of the common stock is not limited. Finally, investors can benefit from a diversified portfolio of common stocks by investing in mutual funds or pension plans. This allows investors to enjoy the return potential offered by stocks while offsetting some of their risk.

Private Equity — There's Nothing Common about It

Private equity is a less familiar and more risky subclass of equity ownership. Private equity represents an investment in a private business. These private businesses do not have stock that trades on public exchanges. The businesses may be mature businesses that have chosen not to become public companies or small growth companies in need of capital. Whatever the case, they look to wealthy individuals or entities that specialize in private equity investing to meet their capital-raising needs. Similar to common stock investing, investors have limited control over the company. However, considering these companies are generally smaller and less established, investors generally are more involved with the business.

Many companies that require private equity investments are in early stages of development and may struggle to achieve profitability. A great many companies fail altogether. As a result, these private companies usually seek relatively sizable investments from a manageable group of investors. Private equity investors are generally knowledgeable in the specific area of business they are investing in. They also have ample resources and can afford relatively sizable investments. Since private equity investments are not very liquid (hard to sell) and they involve significant risk, investors are generally entitled to a substantial portion of any profits. The average individual has neither the resources nor the expertise to make private equity investments. For those who have the resources and knowledge base, private equity investing can prove very profitable. For those with considerable capital but limited investing expertise, there are funds that invest exclusively in private equity.

Entrepreneurship — Uncommon Equity

The final subclass of equity investments is entrepreneurship. Most people don't consider starting a business when they think of equity investing. In a sense, people have more faith in others than they have in themselves. Don't get me wrong. I am not suggesting that everyone can or should start a business. I will, however, suggest that it is a much more rewarding and achievable alternative than most people think. I will also submit to you that while entrepreneurship has substantial risks, it can also prove to be the most profitable of all forms of equity investments. Who is the richest man in the world? Billionaire Bill Gates of course. For all of you young folks out there, who is the richest man under the age of 40? Michael Dell... also a billionaire. Who is the richest man who ever lived? Jesus, of course! What do they all have in common? They all made an uncommon choice. They chose to become entrepreneurs.

> *Matt. 4:18-19* "And Jesus, walking by the sea of Galilee, saw two brethren, Simon called Peter, and Andrew his brother, casting a net into the sea: for they were fishers. And He saith unto them, Follow me, and I will make you fishers of men."

Jesus was in the soul-saving business. In fact, He started it. Given that the whole world was given to Him, I am guessing it is a pretty profitable business. But I digress... the point here is simple. The world's wealthiest people generally share one powerful trait: they believe in themselves. It may seem easy, but the truth is that most people don't believe in themselves. Entrepreneurs make the second best investment you can ever make (the first is an investment in a relationship with God); they invest in themselves. God has made an investment of gifts and abilities in every one of us. For some, not all, the best use of your God-given resources is starting your own business.

Equity Strategy

Virtually every investment portfolio should have some percentage of equity investments. The first factor to consider is time horizon. Given equities are a relatively risky type of investment, it is important to have a meaningful period of time over which to invest. Single individuals or young couples may want to own a substantial amount of equity securities. Investment advisors often suggest between 60 and 70 percent of your overall investment portfolio. The appropriate allocation depends on your risk tolerance. While direct ownership of stocks is fairly common, investors more often own equities indirectly through mutual funds or retirement plans. I generally suggest that individuals limit their ownership of individual equities or private equity unless they have substantial investment expertise and substantial time to research and monitor their investments.

Mature investors should also consider placing some percentage of their overall portfolio in equity investments. This is particularly important if you plan to leave an inheritance for your children or other beneficiaries. Nevertheless, the percentage of equity investments in a mature individual's portfolio should be relatively lower and in most cases should not exceed 50 percent. Another consideration is financial position. Equity investing is available to most individuals given the numerous types of affordable indirect investments. However, private equity investing requires substantial resources and is likely limited to more wealthy investors. My strategy for equity investing does not cover entrepreneurship because it is a very personal decision. You are never too young or too old to pursue your own business. However, you must seek God and make a thorough personal assessment before venturing into entrepreneurship.

Real Estate Ownership

In chapter 1 we noted that many of the world's wealthiest individuals derive their wealth from the ownership of real estate. Real estate investors take comfort in the ownership of tangible assets. Real estate is also attractive because it provides a hedge against inflation. Recall that inflation is the reduction of general purchasing power. This is caused by the tendency of asset prices to rise over time. When inflation goes up (which it generally does), the prices of financial assets, such as stocks and bonds, generally fall. Conversely, tangible assets such as real estate rise in value as inflation increases. While real estate prices can be volatile at times, property values tend to be fairly stable. These are just a few of the characteristics that make real estate an attractive complement to a diversified investment portfolio.

I'll let you in on a little secret. If you own a home, you are already a real estate investor. For many readers, owning a home is all the real estate investing they'll ever want or need. However, others may find that the real estate market is just their cup of tea. The decision to invest in real estate will depend in part on your financial position. Moreover, a successful real estate investor must be knowledgeable, patient, and diligent. Armed with these qualities, an investor is sufficiently prepared to tackle the world of real estate investing. To be clear, I am not suggesting that real estate investing is easy. It takes a lot of hard work and planning. However, the barriers to entry are low, and it doesn't take much to get started.

There are various ways to obtain real estate exposure in your portfolio. Investments in real estate are divided broadly into two categories: mortgages or loans secured by properties and the actual properties themselves. The first decision an investor must make is whether to make direct or indirect investments in real estate. An indirect investment allows an individual to contribute capital while leaving the management of real estate assets to other knowledgeable persons. The investor generally owns some type of security or note.

Conversely, a direct investment results in the beneficial ownership of actual property or assets.

Indirect Investment

The most common form of indirect investment is a real estate investment trust, or REIT. Similar to a mutual fund, a REIT brings together a pool of capital to invest in property, mortgages, or both. REITs also allow investors to diversify among geographies as well as types of properties. There are diversified REITs, as well as REITs that invest exclusively in apartments, regional malls, or office buildings. Income generated by the portfolio of assets is divided among shareholders after the manager of the fund receives a fee and covers the necessary expenses. Shares of REITs are traded on public stock exchanges as well as over-the-counter. REITs are far more liquid than owning an actual piece of property and provide diversification for investors. Another option is to invest in real estate limited partnerships. General partners manage the actual investments while limited partners receive a share of the profits. Limited partnerships have little liquidity and partnership agreements can be fairly complicated. Therefore, real estate limited partnerships should only be considered as options for sophisticated investors.

Direct Investment

Direct investments in real estate generally involve more time and money than indirect investments. As you might guess, they often involve more risk as well. Consequently, the returns from direct investing generally outpace the returns of indirect investing. There are various ways to approach direct investing. An individual may invest in residential properties (single family homes, multifamily units, apartment buildings) or commercial properties (warehouses, retail space, office buildings). Investors may choose to buy properties in order to generate cash flow in the form of rents. Alternatively, investors may buy properties on a speculative basis, looking to buy low and sell higher. Finally, investors may choose to rehab properties or develop new properties. Regardless of the method of investment, planning is the key.

The single most important factor in direct real estate investing is location. An investor must identify areas with the potential for rising property valuations. In addition, investors should focus on areas where they can take advantage of favorable demographic trends. For example, as working singles have migrated to the heart of many large cities, once vacant warehouses have been turned into lucrative lofts. Savvy real estate investors identified these trends in the '80s and early '90s. Investments made during these periods have paid off handsomely in the last decade. Whether your interest lies in renting or speculating, substantial research should be done before making an investment.

The next factor one should consider is building a network. Even if you manage a relatively small real estate portfolio, you will need a network of associates. Depending on your method of investing, your network will likely include brokers, inspectors, general contractors, lawyers, and bankers. Your ability to develop meaningful partnerships in these key fields will play a big part in determining your success. An investor should spend as much time researching potential partners and associates as he or she does researching properties. I also suggest you pay your associates well. The profit motive is the most effective tool for ensuring quality service. If you invest in your associates, they will invest in you.

It's important to start small in direct real estate investing. Many inexperienced real estate investors get themselves in trouble by biting off more than they can chew. I have a close friend who is an experienced real estate investor. He shared the following advice with me. He noted that costs are regularly higher than you anticipate. Transactions almost always take longer than you expect to close and properties generally take longer than you anticipate to rent or sell.

If you keep these things in mind, you will plan conservatively and avoid unnecessary risks.

Real Estate Strategy

Most investment portfolios have a portion dedicated to real estate investments. In most cases, it is the individual's personal residence. While it is difficult to make a case that individuals must own real estate in a diversified portfolio, it is one of the best ways to offset the risk of inflation. As your wealth and financial assets increase, real estate becomes even more attractive. This is why wealthy individuals often own substantial amounts of property. However, real estate needn't only be the domain of the wealthy. Many individuals with modest means have created substantial wealth by investing in real estate.

As a general rule of thumb, it is best to invest in speculative real estate in your early years. Investors can take advantage of tax laws to avoid realizing capital gains. Code 1031 (tax-deferred exchange) allows real estate investors to roll the proceeds from the sale of one property into the purchase of a property of greater value without recognizing a gain on the initial sale. As individuals mature, they generally move from saving to consuming. As a result, income-producing properties that generate rents are more desirable during the golden years.

Suitability must be considered before investing in real estate. Real estate investing takes a lot of research and patience. It also requires a strong network of business associates. If you lack any of these requirements or simply feel uncomfortable with the risks associated with real estate investing, consider indirect investing or avoid real estate investing altogether. Real estate investing can be both profitable and rewarding, but it isn't necessary. Real estate investing requires a reasonable amount of financial resources but is more affordable than most people think. Even for those who choose the direct investing route, there are numerous ways to finance real estate transactions. An investor with good credit and a sound plan can significantly reduce the amount of out-of-pocket costs.

I hope that the information and insights that I have provided regarding types of investments and investment strategy have been valuable. While I have attempted to provide a sound framework for evaluating investment alternatives, your ability to become a successful investor will depend largely on your willingness to obtain knowledge regarding investing. Remember, knowledge and faith are the keys to successful investing.

> *Heb. 11:6* "But without faith it is impossible to please Him (God): for he that cometh to God must believe that He is, and that He is a rewarder of them that diligently seek Him."

Start Planting!

Seeds for Your Soil

Showing Results: Matthew 7

1. How does God determine if we are good investors or not?

2. What happens to bad investors?

According to Your Faith: Matthew 9

1. What proceeds faith?

2. Can we always expect others to act on our behalf?

Faith Without Works: James 2

1. Is faith alone enough to please God?

2. What must follow the application of faith?

Add to Your Faith: 2 Pet. 1:1-10

1. Why does God make promises to believers?

2. What qualities must we add to our faith in order to please God?

CONCLUSION

At the age of two, my family moved into a quaint three-bedroom home with a large backyard — just the kind of refuge my mom needed for my older brother and me. Near the back of our property was a small tree that stood about twelve feet high. It was spring and there were beautiful blossoms on the tree. After further investigation, we realized that the tree was an apple tree, but as the season wore on, it failed to produce fruit.

Two years passed, and the Thomas family continued to grow. I had a brand new baby brother and our house had truly become a home. Although everything in our little world seemed to be changing, that stubborn apple tree still had yet to bear fruit. To add insult to injury, our neighbors a couple of doors down had apple trees overflowing with apples. My father, a relatively patient man, decided he would give the tree one more year. But if that tree failed to bear fruit, it would have to take up residence elsewhere.

It was year three when it happened. Those beautiful little blossoms gave way to tiny little apples. Before we knew it, the tree, and subsequently our yard, was overrun with apples. That was nearly three decades ago. And that stubborn apple tree is still producing apples. Someone had the foresight to plant just one seed and the Thomas family has been blessed with an abundant return. Futhermore, the seed required little attention after it was planted. As with all seeds, God granted the increase. There are three lessons that I learned from that little tree that I hope will propel you to a higher level as an investor.

Tend to Your Own Garden

During those early years when our tree failed to produce apples, it was easy to be attracted by the allure of fresh fruit just down the way. The plants always look greener on the other side. However, this is nothing more than a distraction to keep you from planting and tending to your own garden. We must trust that God will provide us with a just reward when we make the proper investment. As 1 Cor. 3:8-9 says, "Now he that planteth and he that watereth are one: and every man shall receive his own reward according to his own labour."

Believers are often times unable to appreciate why unbelievers seem to prosper in the area of wealth generation. The answer is simple. There are spiritual principles that govern our everyday lives. Just like gravity or relativity in the natural realm, there are definite and specific consequences from the application of these spiritual principles. Many unbelievers apply these established principles in their lives and in turn prosper financially. Remember, the Bible says it rains on the just and unjust. That is also why Jesus says in Luke 16:8, "For the children of this world are in their generation wiser than the children of light." The very purpose of this book is to highlight some of these principles and talk about their practical application in the life of the believer.

Don't Confuse Wants and Needs

It was clear that we wanted that little apple tree to produce apples. But over time, I came to the realization that during those early years we hadn't developed a need for the apples. One of the primary challenges that believers face is that we often confuse the things we want with the things we need. A need is something that is necessary for your welfare or the welfare of others. Conversely, a want is something that you would like to have, but isn't a necessity.

We neither planted the tree nor tended to it, yet we expected it to yield its fruit. We wanted results with no effort. We wanted apples because our neighbors had apples. Once the apple tree finally produced apples we learned the difference between wants and needs. Our first harvest was almost completely wiped out by insects. In future years we made investments in the tree. We sprayed it to protect it from insects. We also pruned the dead branches to ensure the tree was strong and would produce healthy fruit. We dreamed of apple pies and other treats. Our willingness to invest in the apple tree turned our want into a need.

Heb. 12:1-2 says, "Wherefore seeing we also are compassed about with so great a cloud of witnesses, let us lay aside every weight, and the sin which doth so easily beset us, and let us run with patience the race that is set before us, looking unto Jesus who is the author and finisher of our faith." The Word of God instructs us to lay aside every weight and sin that besets us. Notice the term *weight* is distinct from *sin*, which is also referenced. The term weight is the Greek word *ogkos* (ong'-kos). It means a bulk or mass. Metaphorically speaking, the scripture is telling us to get rid of anything that would hinder us from doing God's will. We know that sin gets in the way of God's plan. However, some of the things that we want can deter us from enjoying investing success.

As a believer, God will never give you a want until it becomes a need. It doesn't mean that people won't be able to acquire things that they desire. They just won't get them from God! As you fulfill God's plan for your life, you will undoubtedly require more resources. God will increase your substance because your work for Him has created a need. We must constantly seek God so that He will give us righteous desires.

Harvest Time Is Closer Than You Think

It's funny to think that we were one season away from cutting down our apple tree. I later learned that it can take an apple tree seven or more years before it produces fruit. The individual who planted the tree didn't stick around long enough to see it produce fruit. If we hadn't been so fortunate, we would have missed out on all the wonderful fruit that the tree has produced over the years. The lesson is simple. There was never anything wrong with the tree. It merely had to wait for its season. Gal. 6:9 says, "And let us not be weary in well doing: for in due season we shall reap, if we faint not."

Investing is a time-tested pursuit, much like our walk with God. It is easy to become discouraged when it seems as though our investments are not yielding fruit. It is at those trying times that we have to take on the mind of Christ. Christ had a planter mentality. During His earthly ministry He planted seeds of faith that are producing abundant returns to this day. As you work toward becoming the investor God created you to be, embrace this same mentality. You must never allow yourself to become discouraged as you travel down the path God leads you. Know that your harvest is always closer than you think.

An Unlimited Supply

Phil. 4:19 "But my God shall supply all your need according to His riches in glory by Christ Jesus."

It is a spiritual truth that God created you to be an investor. But there are two things that you must remember if you want to become a truly successful investor. First, you must seek God's will for your life. The Word of God tells us that if we seek God and His righteousness (His will), He will give us the things we desire (Matt. 6:33). Second, you must sow into the Kingdom of God. The Word of God tells us that if we work toward the furtherance of His Kingdom, then He will open up the windows of Heaven and pour out blessings on us (Mal. 3:10).

God expects and has commanded us to multiply our resources and produce good fruit throughout the earth. That is what investing is all about. I pray that the Holy Spirit has sown the righteous seed of investing in your life. I also pray that this book has revealed to you God's plan for investing in a comprehensible and practical manner. It has truly been a joy for me to write and I thank you again for sharing in the vision God has given me. We are all fearfully and wonderfully made. Know that God has planted within you everything that you need to be a successful investor. May God bless you and cause you to prosper as you plant the seeds of righteous investing in your life. May the Grace of God be with you until we meet again.

Your Brother in Christ,
Shundrawn A. Thomas

PART IV

$\mathcal{A}$PPENDICES

INVESTMENT
MODULE

Step I: The Cost of Investing — Can You Afford to Invest?

1. Do you currently have outstanding credit card debt or consumer debt (i.e., furniture, store credit accounts, etc.)?
   ○ Yes   ○ No

2. Do you currently have high interest loans, such as personal
   bank loans, second mortgage, student loans, automobile
   loans, etc.?
   ○ Yes   ○ No

3. Do you have a negative net worth?
   ○ Yes   ○ No

4. Have you lived at your current residence for less than one
   year?
   ○ Yes   ○ No

5. Have you been employed by your current employer for less than one year?

   ◯ Yes   ◯ No

Conclusion: If you answered Yes to all (or most) of the preceding questions, it is unlikely that you can afford to invest. You are either carrying too much debt or need more stability in your career or living circumstances. If you answered Yes to questions 1, 2, or 3, you should concentrate on reducing debt. You should begin by paying off the debt that has the highest interest rate. If you answered Yes to questions 4 or 5, you should consider getting settled a bit before venturing out into the wonderful world of investing. In either case you may benefit from completing the assessment module in *Stop Digging!* The module provided in book one is foundational and essential to proceeding with investing. If you answered No to all (or most) of these questions, you can move on to Step II.

Step II: Preparation for Investing — Are You Ready to Invest?

6. Do you pay tithes?

   ◯ Yes   ◯ No

7. Have you developed a personal and/or family budget?

   ◯ Yes   ◯ No

8. Do you regularly contribute to some type of savings account?

   ◯ Yes   ◯ No

9. Do you have a sufficient cash balance in the bank (I recommend a balance large enough to cover at least six months of total living expenses)?

   ◯ Yes   ◯ No

10. Have you researched various investment alternatives?
    ○ Yes   ○ No

Conclusion: If you answered No to all (or most) of the questions, you are not prepared to invest and should take the necessary steps to answer these questions affirmatively.

If you answered Yes to all (or most) of the preceding questions, you are reasonably prepared to invest and can move on to Step III.

Step III: Risk Tolerance — How Do You Feel about Investing?
Please tally your score.

11. What is your level of investing experience?

none	low	medium	high
1	2	3	4

12. How familiar are you with the type of investments discussed in chapters 7, 8, and 9 of this book?

unfamiliar	somewhat familiar	reasonably familiar	very familiar
1	2	3	4

13. Rate your comfort level with taking risk.

uncomfortable	somewhat comfortable	reasonably comfortable	very comfortable
1	2	3	4

14. Rate your interest in an investment that yields very high returns but could result in the complete loss of your contribution.

Not interested		Definitely interested	
1	2	3	4

15. How would you feel about an investment that yields fairly low returns and rarely loses any of your contribution?

Always prefer	usually prefer	sometimes prefer	rarely prefer
1	2	3	4

Key: 5-10 points   = Low Risk Tolerance
     11-15 points = Medium Risk Tolerance
     16-20 points = High Risk Tolerance

Conclusion: This test merely helps to assess your risk tolerance and will become essential when we discuss portfolio allocation.

Step IV: Contributions —
How Much of My Income Should I Invest?

There is no right or wrong answer to this question. However, some answers are better than others. A common recommendation for believers is the 3 by 10 rule: give God 10 percent, save 10 percent and invest 10 percent. I believe this is a good starting point. My personal recommendation is a bit more aggressive. I recommend you give at least 10 percent in tithes, save 10 percent and invest 30 percent. We will call this the Thomas Rule of Investing. My premise is simple: you should invest as much as you spend. If you can discipline yourself to invest as much as you spend, you will likely become a very successful investor.

Step V: Portfolio Allocation — What Should I Invest In?

There is no right or wrong answer to this question either. However, some answers are preferable to others. Your answer will depend on three things. What is your financial position (i.e., how much money do you have and what do you currently own)? What stage of life are you in (i.e., are you young and single, middle-aged, or retired)? What is your tolerance for risk? Since these answers will differ from person to person, I would like to offer a model portfolio. I have designed a model portfolio for married couples between the ages of twenty-eight and forty-five who have a moderate tolerance for risk. I assume a middle-class income, a personal residence, 2.3 kids, and a dog. The Thomas Portfolio suggests that investors put 60 percent in equities, 20 percent in fixed income, and 20 percent in real estate. My definitions for these investment classes are probably more comprehensive than what some individuals are accustomed to, so please reference the accompanying definitions. Your portfolio should differ depending on your individual risk tolerance. This is meant to serve as a benchmark or starting point.

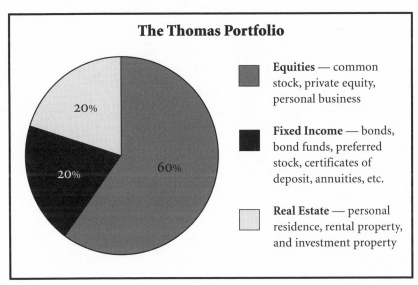

The Thomas Portfolio

20%

20%

60%

Equities — common stock, private equity, personal business

Fixed Income — bonds, bond funds, preferred stock, certificates of deposit, annuities, etc.

Real Estate — personal residence, rental property, and investment property

Step VI — Case Studies

Meet our investing case studies.

- ❧ Reuben Rich — Reuben has been a bus driver for the local transit authority for ten years. He is recently engaged and he is thinking more critically about his financial position.
- ❧ Deborah Dollar — Deborah is a successful young advertising executive. Deborah worked her way through college and has always been prudent when it comes to spending. Deborah currently has a savings account, but she feels as though she should be doing more to secure her financial future.
- ❧ Joseph and Mary Moneybags — Joseph and Mary are young outgoing professionals. They had a picture perfect wedding just after Mary finished medical school. Joseph is an attorney for a corporate law firm, and Mary is a resident at New Jerusalem Memorial Hospital. They've overheard many of their friends talk about the money they've made buying stocks. Joseph and Mary think they should buy stocks also.
- ❧ Adam and Eve Investment — Adam and Eve have been married for ten wonderful years. Adam teaches high school, and Eve stays home with their two lovely children, David and Rebecca, ages four and two. The couple has begun to explore investment options for their children's education.

What do all of these people have in common? They all could use a little investment advice. Let's take a peek at their financial positions and utilize the tools from our investment module to help them develop a personalized investment strategy.

Reuben Rich's Profile

- ❧ Monthly after-tax income: $2,500
- ❧ Rent: $800
- ❧ Car note: $300

- Other household expenses: $600
- Travel and entertainment: $50
- Grocery shopping: $250
- Total monthly expenses: $2,000
- Monthly disposable income: $500
- Savings account balance: $5,000
- Investment balance: $0
- Credit card balance: $0

* Other household expenses include insurance, gasoline, utilities, telephone service, cable service and internet access.

Reuben Rich's Investment Plan

- Reuben is getting married, so the first thing he should do is get together with his fiancée and prepare a budget. Hopefully Reuben has a copy of *Stop Digging!* lying around his apartment. In particular, he needs to assess how much disposable income they will have available.
- Next Reuben should increase his savings before considering other investments. It would be prudent to have about six months worth of monthly expenses in savings before considering other investments.
- After increasing his savings to a comfortable margin, Reuben should consider opening a Roth IRA. It would allow him to contribute up to $3,000 per year. If both he and his wife contribute, they each can contribute $3,000 for a total of $6,000.

Deborah Dollar's Profile

- Monthly after-tax income: $4,000
- Rent: $1,100
- Car note: $350
- Student loan payment: $50

- Other household expenses: $1,000
- Travel and entertainment: $230
- Grocery shopping: $270
- Total monthly expenses: $3,000
- Monthly disposable income: $1,000
- Savings account balance: $12,500
- Investment balance (401k): $9,500
- Student loan balance: $2,000

* Other household expenses include insurance, gasoline, utilities, telephone service, cable service and internet access.

Deborah Dollar's Investment Plan

- Deborah generates a healthy monthly surplus and may want to begin by paying off her student loan.
- Deborah has a healthy savings balance. She should consider investing some or all of her surplus in a long-term investment vehicle that will provide her with capital gains.
- A likely first step would be to increase her contribution to the 401(k) plan offered by her employer. This offers a maximum yearly allotment of $11,000. This investment will offer her the best tax benefit.
- If Deborah still has money remaining, she should next consider investing in a Roth IRA (maximum of $3,000 per year) and then possibly mutual funds. Deborah may also want to seek out a financial advisor to help her with the specific investment selections.

Joseph and Mary Moneybag's Profile

- Monthly after-tax income: $10,000
- Mortgage: $3,000
- Car note(s): $1,500

- Student loan payment(s): $2,400
- Credit card payment(s): $500
- Other household expenses: $1,675
- Travel and entertainment: $700
- Grocery shopping: $475
- Total monthly expenses: $10,250
- Monthly disposable income: -$250
- Savings account balance: $5,000
- Investment balance (401k): $11,500
- Credit card balance (5 cards): $20,000

* Other household expenses include insurance, gasoline, utilities, telephone service, cable service, internet access, housekeeping, lawn care and home security.

Joseph and Mary's Investment Plan
- This appears to be a classic example of overspending. This couple is not ready to invest and likely would have discovered this in Step 1 of our Investment Module.
- This couple should pull out their copy of *Stop Digging!* and work through the modules on budgeting and debt repayment.
- After cutting back on spending, repaying their high interest debt and increasing their savings, they will potentially be ready to invest.

Adam & Eve Investment's Profile
- Monthly net income: $3,370
- Mortgage: $900
- Car note: $270
- Other household expenses: $900
- Travel and entertainment: $250
- Grocery shopping: $550

- Total monthly expenses: $2,870
- Monthly disposable income: $500
- Savings account balance: $17,300
- Investment balance (401k): $57,500
- Credit card balance: $0

* Other household expenses include insurance, gasoline, utilities, telephone service, cable service, internet access, school supplies, and children's allowance.

Adam and Eve's Investment Plan

- Slow and steady wins the race. This couple has been prudent with their spending and is building a solid nest egg. The couple should continue to contribute a modest amount to their savings account each month.
- Adam should also continue to invest in his 401(k) plan offered by his employer. When he receives his regular biannual raise he should increase the amount of his contribution.
- Since their children are very young, they should seek an investment that will provide good capital gains. They might consider opening a 529 educational plan or an educational IRA for each child. Whatever alternative they choose, they should strongly consider investing the contributions in equity mutual funds.

As the case studies demonstrate, investing takes careful consideration and planning. It is essential to complete a financial analysis before venturing into investments. This module introduces a framework for the investment-planning process. Use it to build a complete investment plan.

RECOMMENDED READING LIST

Christian Living

Life on the Edge — A Young Adult's Guide to a Meaningful Future
by Dr. James Dobson
Wild at Heart by John Eldredge
A Woman After God's Own Heart by Elizabeth George
A Man After God's Own Heart by Jim George
Becoming A Leader by Dr. Myles Munroe
Releasing Your Potential by Dr. Myles Munroe
The Power of A Praying Husband by Stormie Omartian
The Power of A Praying Wife by Stormie Omartian

Investing

The Wall Street Journal Guide to Understanding Money and Investing by Kenneth M. Morris & Alan M. Siegel
How to Make Money in Stocks William J. O'Neil
Barron's Guide to Making Investment Decisions by Douglas Sease & John Prestbo

Start Planting!

The Craft of Investing by John Train
Personal Finance for Dummies by Eric Tyson

General Business/Business Principles
God is My CEO by Larry Julian
Rich Dad Poor Dad by Robert T. Kiyosaki
Dig Your Well Before You're Thirsty by Harvey Mackay
Decision Traps by J. Edward Russo & Paul J. H. Schoemaker
The Millionaire Next Door by Thomas J. Stanley, Ph.D. & William
    D. Danko, Ph.D.

Other
Extraordinary Delusions and the Madness of Crowds by Charles
    Mackay

Business Periodicals
Money Magazine
Barron's
Fortune
Black Enterprise

Epilogue

Six years ago I found myself at an interesting crossroad. I had just spent several years working in New York City for a major Wall Street firm. I had decided to further my education and was preparing to begin studies at the University of Chicago's Graduate School of Business. I had recently married my lovely wife, Latania, and we were returning home to Chicago. Although I was relatively successful in the early part of my career, I didn't feel complete. I'd turned my back on God and the void that was left could not be filled by my career. I knew what was missing, and it was the proper relationship with God.

Upon returning home and submitting myself to the leadership of my parents, Pastors Gary and Audrey Thomas, my life began to improve dramatically. I rededicated my life to Christ and began to immerse myself in my studies. I was literally going back to school in every aspect of my life. I spent the next two years working on my MBA. Likewise, I spent the same period of time working on my spiritual development and character. I grew more confident in my abilities as a business professional, but more importantly I gained confidence in my walk with God.

About the time I completed my graduate course work, God began to deal with me more intimately. I had matured to a point where He could show me some things about myself that weren't easy to accept. God revealed to me that while I had changed certain behaviors, I hadn't truly changed my thinking. I had always been a very disciplined individual so I was comfortable conforming to certain behaviors. God told me that He wanted to completely change my life for the better, and in order to do that He had to change my way of thinking.

> *Rom. 12:2* "And be not conformed to this world: but be ye transformed by the renewing of your mind."

One of the areas that God dealt with me was concerning money. My wife and I had earned both undergraduate and graduate degrees in finance and accounting. We each had established careers in financial services. I figured we were well prepared to deal with any issues concerning money. How many people know God knows infinitely more than we know about any and everything? How many people know that in all our ways we must acknowledge God if we want to have success? God asked me a very simple question. How well has your financial system worked for you?

> *Prov. 3:6* "In all thy ways acknowledge him, and he shall direct thy paths."

As I began to take inventory of my personal finances, I realized the picture wasn't as pretty as I thought. Although I had benefited from some savings and financial assistance, I completed the program with over $40,000 worth of student loans. Don't cry for me, I was one of the lucky ones. I had also accumulated another $10,000 of credit card debt. My wife and I had just signed a contract to purchase a new home and actually were delighted that they only asked us to come up with 5 percent of the value of the home. (It didn't really dawn on me that the bank owned the other 95 percent.) Furthermore, I persuaded her that there was no reason to move into an empty house, so we gladly accepted Household Financial's offer to extend us a bit of credit to buy furniture. Now I don't want to disclose too much of my personal business, but if you throw in the car lease (yes, that's a form of debt) and my hefty mortgage, we literally owed hundreds of thousands worth of debt.

I got honest with myself and admitted that I did not have the best financial plan. While I believed myself to be disciplined and prudent, my successful lifestyle seemed to result in increasing debt and hardship. In some respects, I had bought into the world's illusion of prosperity. I asked God for direction and some may be surprised with what He told me. The first thing God instructed me to do was to pay my tithes. I was about to return to work and God had blessed me with a tremendous job opportunity working for another Wall Street firm. This job was truly a blessing because I was able to work out of the Chicago office and stay close to both my natural family and my church family. God reminded me that while on my first job, I never once paid tithes. I earned tens of thousands of dollars and kept it all to myself. God showed me that I was unable to truly prosper because I didn't have the right perspective when it came to money.

> *Prov. 19:21* "There are many devices (plans) in a man's heart (mind); nevertheless the counsel of the Lord, that shall stand."

God instructed me that He was not merely looking for a financial tithe, but was also looking for a tithe of my time. He expected me to put His will first as opposed to just worrying about my own agenda. From my very first check I vowed that I would pay God first and I haven't missed a payment yet. As I began to buy into God's financial plan, He began to overhaul mine. My wife has always been frugal when it comes to money. God began to use her to teach me more personal discipline. She paid off ten years worth of school loans in three short years and encouraged me to make debt reduction a top priority. She also developed a budget for herself and encouraged us to develop our first household budget. Rather than drive, we took the bus or train to work. She packed a bag lunch as opposed to paying for lunch at work. People we worked with laughed at some of our tactics, but we were benefiting from prudent spending and shrewd financial management.

> *Prov. 10:4* "He becometh poor that dealeth with a slack hand: but the hand of the diligent maketh rich."

Once I made God a priority, He began to reveal to me numerous things in His Word concerning finances. I learned the appropriate attitude toward debt, insurance, and investing from His Word. This also enabled me to appropriately apply the practical knowledge found in other books. Right before my eyes, God was changing my thinking. I realized that His Word had empowered me to destroy my digger mentality. God replaced poor habits and behaviors with prudent judgment and sound decisions. In four short years since completion of my graduate degree, God has revolutionized my thinking, both spiritually and financially.

I am sure that some are wondering about my current financial position and investing success. I will share a few tidbits without getting myself into trouble on the home front. Over the past four years, God has enabled our family to pay off nearly $200,000 worth of debt. This has included paying off all of our school loans as well as paying off a five-year automobile loan in just fifteen months. We were blessed to pay cash for our second automobile, so now we drive worry free. The only debt that we have remaining is our home mortgage and it has been greatly reduced. God willing, we plan to pay it off in the very near future. We are aggressive savers and investors. Our savings and investments have grown exponentially and our net worth is approximately four times our annual salary. Finally, God has given my extended family the vision to start and finance our own business. This book is just one of the many products that will result from that vision.

What I've shared is only a fraction of what I believe God can accomplish in the financial lives of believers. I've shared my personal experience to highlight what God has done in my life and not to highlight anything that I've done. I am convinced that the principles of God are essential to sound stewardship and successful investing. My prayer is that the same revelations that God has shared with me become a reality in the life of every believer. Admittedly, I have yet to fully become the investor that God has purposed me to be. However, I can truly say that His grace has enabled me to *Stop Digging!* and *Start Planting!* May God's grace afford you the same experience and may all your needs be supplied according to His riches through Christ Jesus.

Yours in Christ,
Shundrawn A. Thomas

ABOUT THE AUTHOR

Shundrawn A. Thomas, a native and resident of Chicago, Illinois, is a licensed investment professional with extensive Wall Street experience. Shundrawn is a gifted teacher, minister, motivational speaker, author, entrepreneur, husband and father. Most recently, he worked as a vice president for a leading investment banking firm where he gained extensive experience in equities, fixed income, and derivative investment products. His strong business acumen and passion for financial markets have made him an invaluable advisor. Shundrawn is widely respected by his professional colleagues for his dedication to excellence and his principled business approach.

Currently, Shundrawn serves as managing partner and chief operating officer of Adelphos Holdings LLC, a knowledge-based holding company. The company's primary businesses include book publishing, publishing services, and advisory services. Shundrawn and long-time friend Cliff Goins iv are the co-founders of the company. The two have begun taking their message to the world in the two-part book series *Stop Digging!* and *Start Planting!*

Shundrawn is currently a minister and board member of Look Up & Live Full Gospel Ministries. He also serves in various other capacities, including financial advisor and adult Sunday school teacher. Shundrawn participates in a wealth of volunteer projects in and around the Chicago area. His community involvement has given him the opportunity to speak at local churches and schools on subjects including education, investing, and Christian living.

Shundrawn holds a bachelor of science in accounting from Florida A&M University. He also holds a masters of business administration from the University of Chicago's Graduate School of Business with concentrations in finance and accounting. Shundrawn has obtained his series 7, series 63, and series 3 securities licenses. Additionally, he is a Level ii candidate for the Chartered Financial Analyst program. Shundrawn is happily married and enjoys spending time with his wife, Latania, and their son, Javon. When he's not on the go, Shundrawn enjoys reading, physical fitness, and college football.

What Do You Think?

We want your input — help make our products better!

Log on to http://www.StopStartBooks.com now!
The interface is easy and you'll receive tons of FREE and useful information.

Give us feedback on:

〜 Book content 〜

〜 Book relevance 〜

〜 Book design and layout 〜

〜 Suggestions for future titles 〜

〜 Any other comments you may have 〜

There's More at StopStartBooks.com!
At StopStartBooks.com you can discover great new products for yourself, family and friends.